1001 ESSENTIAL SENTENCES
FOR ELEMENTARY ENGLISH LEARNERS

CEDU 쎄듀는 A **C**omprehensive **E**nglish e**DU**cation(종합적 영어교육)의 약자입니다.

펴낸이	김기훈 · 김진희
펴낸곳	(주)쎄듀 / 서울시 강남구 논현로 305 (역삼동)
발행일	2016년 11월 28일 초판 1쇄
내용문의	www.cedubook.com
구입문의	콘텐츠 마케팅 사업본부
	Tel. 02-6241-2007
	Fax. 02-2058-0209
등록번호	제 22-2472호
ISBN	978-89-6806-080-9

초등코치
천일문
sentence

세이펜과
초등코치 천일문 Sentence의 만남!

✦ ✦ ✦

〈초등코치 천일문 Sentence〉는 세이펜이 적용된 도서입니다.
세이펜을 영어에 가져다 대기만 하면 원어민이 들려주는 생생한 영어 발음과
억양을 바로 확인할 수 있습니다.

*세이펜은 본 교재에 포함되어 있지 않습니다.
기존에 보유하신 세이펜이 있다면 핀파일만 다운로드해서 바로 이용하실 수 있습니다.
단, Role-Play 기능은 SBS-1000 이후 모델에서만 구동됩니다.

🖊 세이펜을 대면 해당 words & chunks를 두 번씩 들을 수 있습니다.

🖊 말풍선 안에 대면 정답을 포함한 문장 전체를 두 번씩 들을 수 있습니다.

🖊 각 그림에 대면 해당 문장을 두 번씩 들을 수 있습니다.

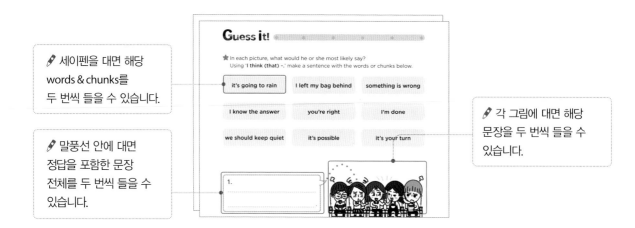

🖊 각 문장에 대면 원어민의 정확한 발음과 억양을 들을 수 있습니다.

🖊 〈보기〉나 번호에 대면 상자 안 대화 전체를 들을 수 있습니다.

🖊 녹음 버튼🎙에 댄 후 정답이 들어갈 문장을 녹음할 수 있습니다. 이때 정답을 포함한 문장 전체를 녹음하세요.

🖊 재생 버튼▷에 대면 자신이 녹음한 문장을 바로 들어볼 수 있습니다.

🖊 빈칸에 대면 정답을 포함한 문장 전체를 들을 수 있습니다.

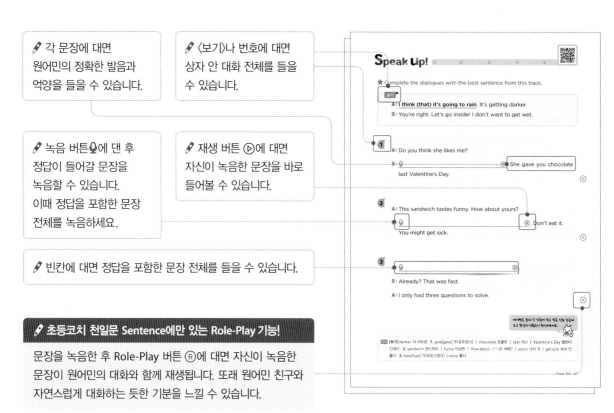

🖊 초등코치 천일문 Sentence에만 있는 Role-Play 기능!

문장을 녹음한 후 Role-Play 버튼 ®에 대면 자신이 녹음한 문장이 원어민의 대화와 함께 재생됩니다. 또래 원어민 친구와 자연스럽게 대화하는 듯한 기분을 느낄 수 있습니다.

| WORKBOOK |

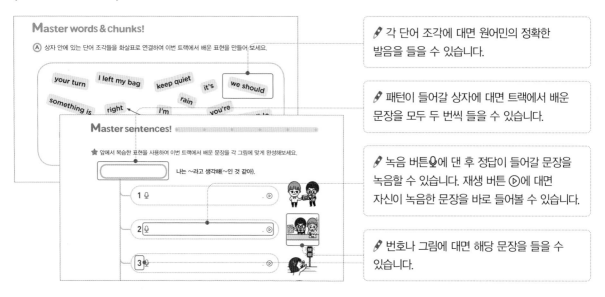

🖊 각 단어 조각에 대면 원어민의 정확한 발음을 들을 수 있습니다.

🖊 패턴이 들어갈 상자에 대면 트랙에서 배운 문장을 모두 두 번씩 들을 수 있습니다.

🖊 녹음 버튼🎙에 댄 후 정답이 들어갈 문장을 녹음할 수 있습니다. 재생 버튼▷에 대면 자신이 녹음한 문장을 바로 들어볼 수 있습니다.

🖊 번호나 그림에 대면 해당 문장을 들을 수 있습니다.

How to Study with Saypen

세이펜으로 이렇게 공부해 보세요!

*번역 기능 | 세이펜으로 책을 찍어서 원어민 음성을 들은 후, Ⓣ 버튼을 짧게 누르면 해석 음원을 들을 수 있습니다.

✏️ 세이펜을 대면 패턴이 들어간 문장을 A부터 차례대로 두 번씩 들을 수 있습니다.

✏️ 각 그림이나 상자에 대면 해당 문장을 두 번씩 들을 수 있습니다.

✏️ 재생 버튼 ⓟ에 대면 모든 문장이 두 번씩 재생됩니다.

✏️ 문장 번호나 문장에 대면 해당 문장을 두 번씩 들을 수 있습니다.

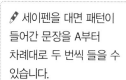

✏️ 게임 (OFF)일 때 각 그림이나 영어에 대면 해당 words & chunks를 두 번씩 들을 수 있습니다.

✏️ 게임 (OFF)일 때 재생 버튼 ⓟ에 대면 모든 words & chunks가 두 번씩 재생됩니다. (왼쪽 → 오른쪽)

✏️ 게임 (OFF)일 때 문장에 대면 해당 문장을 두 번씩 들을 수 있습니다.

✏️ 시작 버튼 (ON)에 대면 퀴즈를 시작할 수 있습니다. (두 종류의 퀴즈를 풀어볼 수 있습니다.) 종료 시에는 종료 버튼 (OFF)를 누릅니다.

✏️ 게임 (ON)일 때 〈Quiz 1〉 각 그림이나 영어에 대면 해당 words & chunks가 재생됩니다. 이것을 듣고 아래 문장 중 알맞은 빈칸을 선택하면 정답음이 나옵니다.

✏️ 게임 (ON)일 때 〈Quiz 2〉 재생 버튼 ⓟ에 대면 words & chunks가 랜덤으로 재생됩니다. 이것을 듣고 아래 문장 중 알맞은 빈칸을 선택하면 정답음이 나옵니다.

초등코치 천일문 시리즈
with 세이펜

| 원어민 음성 실시간 반복학습 | 녹음 기능으로 쉐도잉 발음교정 | 게임 기능으로 재미있고 유익하게 | Role-Play로 자신감까지 Up |

초등코치 천일문 시리즈 Sentence 1권~5권, Grammar 1권~3권, Voca&Story 1권~2권 모두 세이펜을 활용하여 원어민 MP3 음성 재생 서비스를 이용할 수 있습니다.

(책 앞면 하단에 세이펜 로고 **SAYPEN TV**가 있습니다.)

세이펜 핀파일 다운로드 안내

STEP ① 세이펜과 컴퓨터를 USB 케이블로 연결하세요.

STEP ② 쎄듀북 홈페이지(www.cedubook.com)에 접속 후, 학습자료실 메뉴에서 학습할 교재를 찾아 이동합니다.

> 초·중등교재 ▶ 구문 ▶ 학습교재 클릭 ▶ 세이펜 핀파일 자료 클릭
> ▶ 다운로드 (저장을 '다른 이름으로 저장'으로 변경하여 저장소를 USB로 변경) ▶ 완료

STEP ③ 음원 다운로드가 완료되면 세이펜과 컴퓨터의 USB 케이블을 분리하세요.

STEP ④ 세이펜을 분리하면 "시스템을 초기화 중입니다. 잠시만 기다려 주세요" 라는 멘트가 나옵니다.

STEP ⑤ 멘트 종료 후 세이펜을 〈초등코치 천일문 Sentence〉 표지의 제목 부분에 대보세요.
효과음이 나온 후 바로 학습을 시작할 수 있습니다.

참고사항

◆ 세이펜에서 제작된 모든 기종(기존에 보유하고 계신 기종도 호환 가능)으로 사용이 가능합니다. 단, Sentence 교재의 Role-Play 기능은 레인보우 SBS-1000 기종에서만 구동됩니다. (신규 구매자는 SBS-1000 이후 모델의 구매를 권장합니다.)

◆ 모든 기종은 세이펜에서 권장하는 최신 펌웨어 업데이트를 진행해 주시기 바랍니다.
업데이트는 세이펜 홈페이지(www.saypen.com)에서 가능합니다.

◆ 초등코치 천일문 시리즈의 핀파일은 쎄듀북 홈페이지(www.cedubook.com)와 세이펜 홈페이지(www.saypen.com)에서 모두 다운로드 가능합니다.

◆ 세이펜을 이용하지 않는 학습자는 쎄듀북 홈페이지 부가학습자료, 교재 내 QR코드 이미지 등을 활용하여 원어민 음성으로 학습하실 수 있습니다.

◆ 기타 문의사항은 www.cedubook.com / 02-3272-4766으로 연락 바랍니다.

초등코치

천일문
sentence

✦ ✦ ✦

5

저자

김기훈

現 ㈜ 쎄듀 대표이사
現 메가스터디 영어영역 대표강사
前 서울특별시 교육청 외국어 교육정책자문위원회 위원

저서 천일문 / 천일문 Training Book / 천일문 GRAMMAR / 초등코치 천일문
어법끝 / 어휘끝 / 첫단추 / 쎈쓰업 / 파워업 / 빈칸백서 / 오답백서
쎄듀 본영어 / 문법의 골든룰 101 / ALL씀 서술형 / 수능실감
거침없이 Writing / Grammar Q / Reading Q / Listening Q
왓츠 그래머 / 왓츠 리딩 / 패턴으로 말하는 초등 필수 영단어 등

쎄듀 영어교육연구센터

쎄듀 영어교육센터는 영어 콘텐츠에 대한 전문지식과 경험을 바탕으로
최고의 교육 콘텐츠를 만들고자 최선의 노력을 다하는 전문가 집단입니다.

인지영 선임연구원 **· 장혜승** 전임연구원

검토위원

성윤선

現 Charles G. Emery Elementary School 교사

약력 하버드대학교 교육대학원 Language and Literacy 석사
이화여자대학교 교육공학, 영어교육 복수 전공
가톨릭대학교 교수학습센터 연구원
이화여자대학교 교수학습개발원 연구원
한국교육개발원 연구원

마케팅	콘텐츠 마케팅 사업본부
영업	문병구
제작	정승호
인디자인 편집	올댓에디팅
표지 디자인	윤혜영, 이연수
내지 디자인	에피그램
영문교열	Eric Scheusner

Foreword

〈초등코치 천일문 SENTENCE〉 시리즈를 펴내며

초등 영어, 무엇을 어떻게 시작해야 할까요?

자녀에게 영어 공부를 시키는 목적은 여러 가지일 것입니다. '우리 아이가 원어민처럼 영어를 잘했으면 좋겠다', '생활하는 데 영어가 걸림돌이 되지 않으면 좋겠다'라는 바람에서, 또는 중학교 내신이나 대학 입시를 위해 영어 공부를 시키기도 하지요.

영어를 공부하는 목표가 무엇이 되든, 영어의 기초가 잡혀 있지 않으면 새로운 것을 배우는 데 시간과 노력이 더 많이 들 수밖에 없습니다. 그리고 영어는 아이가 공부해야 하는 단 하나의 과목이 아니기에, 영어 공부에 비교적 많은 시간을 투자할 수 있는 초등학생 시기가 매우 중요하지요.

〈초등코치 천일문 SENTENCE〉 시리즈는 기초를 세우기에 가장 적절한 초등학생 시기에 **1,001개 통문장 암기로 영어의 기초를 완성**할 수 있도록 기획되었습니다. 1,001개 문장은 꼭 알아야 할 패턴 112개와 실생활에 유용한 표현들로 구성되었습니다.

| 문장과 덩어리 표현(chunk)이 학습의 주가 됩니다.

영어를 학습할 때는 문장(full sentence)과 덩어리 표현(chunk) 학습법이 더욱 효과적입니다. 〈초등코치 천일문 SENTENCE〉는 우리말 설명을 최소화하고 문장 자체에 집중할 수 있도록 구성했습니다. 책에 수록된 모든 문장과 표현, 대화는 現 미국 공립 초등학교 선생님의 검토를 받아 완성되었습니다.

| 문장 암기를 쉽게 할 수 있도록 설계했습니다.

문장과 표현이 자연스럽게 7번 반복되어 책을 따라 하다 보면 자동으로 1,001개 문장을 암기할 수 있습니다. 그리고 이해와 기억을 돕기 위해 재미있는 그림으로 새로운 표현들과 상황을 제시했습니다. 또한, 대부분 문장의 주어를 '나(I)'로 하여 아이들이 실생활에서도 자주 말하고 쓸 수 있도록 했습니다.

1,001개 통문장 암기로 탄탄한 기초가 세워지면, 내신, 수능, 말하기·듣기 등 앞으로의 모든 영어 학습에 대한 불안감이 해소될 것입니다. 〈초등코치 천일문 SENTENCE〉 시리즈와의 만남을 통해 영어 학습이 더욱더 쉬워지고 즐거워지는 경험을 꼭 할 수 있기를 희망합니다.

저 자

추천의 글

외국어 학습은 수년의 시간이 수반되는 장거리 경주입니다. 따라서, 잘못된 방식으로 학습을 시작해 외국어 학습의 즐거움을 초반에 잃어버리면, 끝까지 지속하지 못하고 중도에 포기하게 됩니다. 쎄듀의 초등코치 천일문은 대한민국의 초등 영어 학습자들이 효과적이고 효율적으로 영어학습의 경주를 시작할 수 있도록 여러분의 걸음을 친절하고 꼼꼼하게 안내해 줍니다.

효과적인 초등 영어 학습을 약속합니다.

영어 학습 과정에서 단어를 하나하나 익히는 것도 물론 중요하지만, 덩어리(chunk) 또는 패턴으로 다양한 영어 표현을 익히면 영어를 보다 유창하게 구사하고, 빠른 속도로 이해할 수 있습니다. 쎄듀의 초등코치 천일문은 일상 생활에서 가장 빈번히 사용되는 112개의 문장 패턴을 담았습니다.

또한, 각 문장 패턴당 8~9개의 훈련 문장들과 함께 4개의 짧은 대화가 수록되어 해당 패턴을 실제로 어떻게 사용할 수 있는지 보여줍니다. 이렇게 다양한 예문과 구체적인 대화 상황을 제시함으로써 쎄듀 초등코치 천일문은 언어 학습에 필수적인 패턴을 활용한 반복 학습을 이루어 갑니다.

112개의 필수 영어 문장 패턴과 이를 활용한 1,001개의 예문 학습, 그리고 구석구석 꼼꼼하게 안내된 어휘 학습 까지. 쎄듀의 초등코치 천일문은 영어 학습을 시작하는 학생들이 탄탄한 영어의 기초를 다질 수 있는 효과적인 학습방법을 제시합니다.

효율적인 초등 영어 학습을 약속합니다.

애써 영어 공부를 했는데, 실제 영어를 사용하는 현장에서 활용할 수 없다면 어떻게 해야 할까요? 기존의 학습 내용을 지우고, 출발점으로 돌아가 다시 시작해야 합니다. 장거리를 달려야 하는데 다시 시작이라니 지칠 수밖에 없습니다.

쎄듀의 초등코치 천일문은 한 문장 한 문장, 대화 하나하나를 미국 초등학생들이 실제로 사용하는지 철저히 고려하여 엄선된 내용을 채택하였습니다. 초등학생들의 관심 주제를 바탕으로 문장과 대화들이 작성되어 학습자 모두 내용을 친숙하게 느낄 수 있습니다.

친숙한 대화 소재를 바탕으로 한 실제적인 영어 예문 학습을 통해, 본 교재를 이용한 학생들은 잘못된 공부로 인한 소진 없이 효율적으로 영어의 기본기를 다질 수 있습니다.

LA에서, 성윤선

Series

1권 Track 01~24 001~212	2권 Track 25~48 213~428	3권 Track 49~70 429~624	4권 Track 71~91 625~813	5권 Track 92~112 814~1001
This is ~.	I can ~.	I'm going to ~.	I started -ing.	Give me ~.
That's ~.	I can't ~.	He[She]'s going to ~.	I began to ~.	He[She] gave me ~.
I am a/an ~.	You can ~.	Are you going to ~?	Stop -ing.	I'll show you ~.
I am ~.	Can I ~?	I was about to ~.	I[We] kept -ing.	I'll tell you ~.
I'm not ~.	Can you ~?	I'm -ing.	I want to ~.	It makes me ~.
You are ~.	I[You] should ~.	He[She]'s -ing.	I don't want to ~.	He[She, It] made me ~.
He[She] is ~.	You must ~.	Are you -ing?	I wanted to ~.	Let me ~.
He[She] is in ~.	I[You] might ~.	I was -ing.	I like to ~.	Help me ~.
It is ~.	I have to ~.	What's ~?	I need to ~.	I want you to ~.
Are you ~?	You have to ~.	What do you ~?	I tried to ~.	I saw him[her] -ing.
It's ~.	You don't have to ~.	What are you -ing?	I'm supposed to ~.	I heard him[her] -ing.
There is ~.	I had to ~.	Who is ~?	It's time to ~.	I think (that) ~.
There are ~.	I used to ~.	Why do you ~?	Do you know how to ~?	I don't think (that) ~.
Is[Are] there any ~?	I was ~.	Why don't we ~?	I don't know what to ~.	I thought (that) ~.
There's no ~.	He[She] was ~.	Where is ~?	He[She] seems to ~.	I know (that) ~.
I have ~.	I went to ~.	Where did you ~?	You look ~.	I knew (that) ~.
He[She] has ~.	I put it ~.	How do you ~?	I feel ~.	I don't know what ~.
I want ~.	I didn't ~.	When are you going to ~?	I got ~.	I guess (that) ~.
I like ~.	Did you ~?	What a[an] ~!	I'm getting ~.	I hope (that) ~.
I hate ~.	I[We] will ~.	Do[Be] ~.	He[She] seems ~.	I'm sure (that) ~.
I need ~.	He[She] will ~.	Don't ~.	It looks like ~.	That's why ~.
I don't ~.	I won't ~.	Let's ~.		
Do you ~?	I'll be able to ~.			
Does he[she] ~?	Will you ~?			

Preview

Step 1

대표 문장과 패턴을 확인합니다.
미국 도서관 협회 추천 영어 동화책을 분석하여 가장 많이 쓰이는 패턴 112가지를 쉽고 간략한 설명과 함께 여러 예문으로 제시했습니다.

QR코드

휴대폰을 통해 QR 코드를 인식하면, 본문의 모든 문장, 단어 및 청크, 대화의 MP3 파일이 재생됩니다.

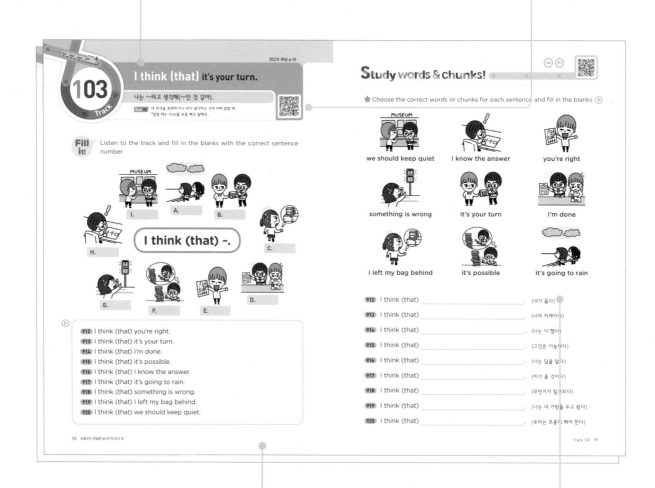

Step 2

미국 현지 초등학생 원어민 성우들이 읽는 문장들을 듣고 그림과 연결합니다.
귀로 듣고 눈으로 보면서 직접 패턴과 청크들을 연결합니다. 보기와 듣기까지 동시에 함으로써 학습 내용을 오래 기억할 수 있습니다.

Step 3

단어와 청크를 집중적으로 연습합니다.
단어와 청크 뜻에 맞는 그림을 연결해 보면서 문장을 완성합니다. 실생활에서 자주 쓸 수 있는 유용한 표현들을 익힐 수 있습니다.

Step 4

각 그림 상황에 알맞은 문장을 완성합니다.

앞에서 배운 패턴과 청크를 사용하여 완전한 문장을 써 봅니다. 재미있는 그림을 통해 문장이 실제로 사용되는 상황을 알 수 있습니다.

Step 5

각 대화 상황에 알맞은 문장을 넣어 봅니다.

학습한 문장이 실제로 어떤 대화 상황에서 쓰일 수 있는지 확실하게 알 수 있습니다.

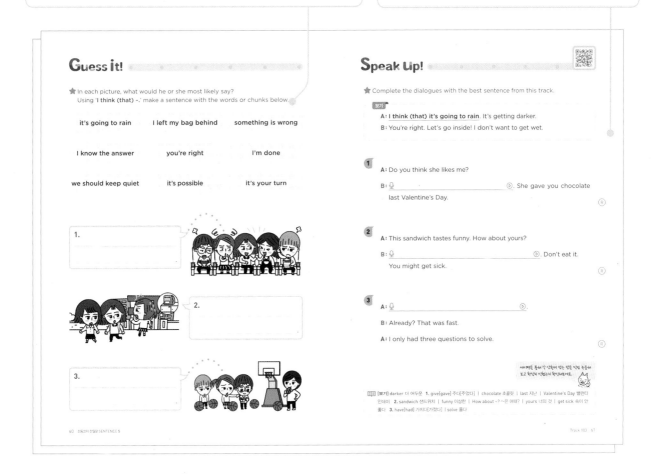

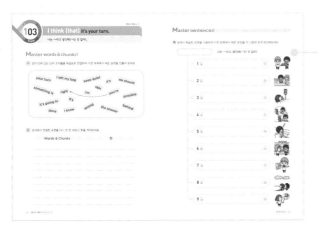

Step 6

워크북으로 단어 및 청크, 문장을 마스터합니다.

Step 7

무료 부가서비스 자료로 완벽하게 복습합니다.

1. 어휘리스트 2. 어휘테스트 3. 본문 해석 연습지
4. 본문 말하기·영작 연습지   5. MP3 파일

* 모든 자료는 www.cedubook.com에서 다운로드 가능합니다.

MP3 활용하기

〈초등코치 천일문 SENTENCE〉 부가서비스 자료에는 본문의 모든 문장, 단어 및 청크, 대화의 MP3 파일이 들어 있습니다.

• 미국 현지 초등학생 원어민 성우의 생생하고 정확한 발음과 억양을 확인할 수 있습니다.

• 문장은 2회씩 녹음되어 있습니다.

Strong Points

1 20일 또는 16일 완성

〈초등코치 천일문 SENTENCE〉 시리즈는 한 권을 20일 또는 16일 동안 학습할 수 있도록 구성되어 있습니다. 아이의 상황에 맞게 계획표를 선택하여 학습할 수 있습니다.

2 복잡한 문법 설명 없이도 가능한 학습

어렵고 복잡한 문법 용어를 설명할 필요가 없습니다. 패턴과 문장 자체의 의미를 받아들이는 데 집중하도록 구성되어 부담 없이 학습해 나갈 수 있습니다.

3 문장이 자연스럽게 외워지는 자동 암기 시스템

각 트랙에는 8~9개의 문장이 수록되어 있습니다. 본책과 워크북에는 이러한 문장들과 문장 속 표현들이 7번이나 자연스럽게 반복되는 효과가 있어서 책을 따라 하다 보면 자동적으로 암기가 가능합니다.

★ MP3 파일을 반복해서 들으면 암기에 더욱 효과적입니다.
책에 실린 모든 문장은 초등학생 원어민 성우 Arthur와 Claire가 미국 현지에서 녹음했습니다.

🖊 세이펜으로 더 쉽게, 더 자주 반복해서 들을 수 있습니다.
또한, Study words & chunks의 게임 기능을 통해 더욱 재미있게 암기할 수 있습니다.

4 이해와 기억을 돕는 1,337개의 그림

그림과 상황을 통해 문장의 의미를 직관적으로 이해할 수 있도록 1,001개의 표현을 묘사한 그림과 336개의 대화 상황을 나타내는 그림을 실었습니다.

my mistake

⑤ 또래 원어민 친구와 나눠보는 대화

각 트랙의 마지막 페이지에는 학습한 문장을 채워볼 수 있는 dialogue 4개가 실려 있습니다. 이 대화는 모두 뉴욕에 거주하는 초등학생 원어민 성우 Eden과 Kara가 미국 현지에서 녹음 한 것으로, A와 B 중 골라서 role playing을 할 수 있습니다. 꾸준히 연습하다 보면, 실제로 원어 민 친구를 만나도 당황하지 않고 자연스럽게 대화할 수 있습니다.

세이펜의 Role-Play 기능을 활용하여 더욱 생생한 대화를 경험해 볼 수 있습니다.
세이펜으로 각 dialogue의 빈칸을 포함한 문장 전체를 녹음한 후 Role-Play 버튼 ⓡ에 대면,
녹음한 문장이 원어민의 대화와 함께 자연스럽게 재생됩니다.

⑥ 다양한 부가 학습 자료로 완벽 복습

1,001개의 문장을 다양한 부가 학습 자료로 완벽하게 복습할 수 있습니다. 테스트 자료로도 유용 하게 활용하실 수 있습니다.
(www.cedubook.com에서 무료로 다운로드 가능합니다.)

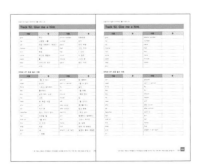

어휘리스트 & 어휘테스트
본문에 실린 모든 어휘를 학습할 수 있습니다. 어휘리스트로 학습한 후에는 어휘테스트로 어 휘 실력을 점검해볼 수 있습니다.

본문 해석 연습지
1,001개 문장의 해석을 써보며 의미를 복습할 수 있습니다.

본문 말하기·영작 연습지
우리말 해석을 보고 영어로 바꿔 말하 거나 써볼 수 있습니다. 말하기·영작 연습지는 '우리말 뜻을 보고 빈칸 채우기 ▶ 순서대로 어휘 배 열하기 ▶ 뜻을 보며 영작하기'의 순서 로 구성되어 있습니다.

Contents 📖

〈초등코치 천일문 SENTENCE 5〉 목차

책속책 WORKBOOK | 정답과 해설

Study Plan

★ **20일 완성!**

	Track	공부한 날짜	
1일차	Track 92, 워크북/Track 93, 워크북	월	일
2일차	Track 94, 워크북/Track 95, 워크북	월	일
3일차	Track 92~93 Review	월	일
4일차	Track 94~95 Review	월	일
5일차	Track 96, 워크북/Track 97, 워크북	월	일
6일차	Track 98, 워크북/Track 99, 워크북	월	일
7일차	Track 96~97 Review	월	일
8일차	Track 98~99 Review	월	일
9일차	Track 100, 워크북/Track 101, 워크북	월	일
10일차	Track 102, 워크북/Track 103, 워크북	월	일
11일차	Track 100~101 Review	월	일
12일차	Track 102~103 Review	월	일
13일차	Track 104, 워크북/Track 105, 워크북	월	일
14일차	Track 106, 워크북/Track 107, 워크북	월	일
15일차	Track 104~105 Review	월	일
16일차	Track 106~107 Review	월	일
17일차	Track 108, 워크북/Track 109, 워크북	월	일
18일차	Track 110, 워크북/Track 111, 워크북/Track 112, 워크북	월	일
19일차	Track 108~109 Review	월	일
20일차	Track 110~112 Review	월	일

★ 16일 완성!

	Track	공부한 날짜	
1일차	Track 92~93, 워크북	월	일
2일차	Track 94~95, 워크북	월	일
3일차	Track 96~97, 워크북	월	일
4일차	Track 92~94 Review	월	일
5일차	Track 95~97 Review	월	일
6일차	Track 98~99, 워크북	월	일
7일차	Track 100~101, 워크북	월	일
8일차	Track 102~103, 워크북	월	일
9일차	Track 98~100 Review	월	일
10일차	Track 101~103 Review	월	일
11일차	Track 104~106, 워크북	월	일
12일차	Track 104~106 Review	월	일
13일차	Track 107~109, 워크북	월	일
14일차	Track 107~109 Review	월	일
15일차	Track 110~112, 워크북	월	일
16일차	Track 110~112 Review	월	일

Let's Start!

92

Track

Give me a hint.

나에게 ~을 줘.

Say It! 상대방에게 무엇을 달라고 요청할 때

Fill it! Listen to the track and fill in the blanks with the correct sentence number.

I.

A.

B.

H.

Give me ~.

C.

G.

F.

E.

D.

814 Give me a call.	**819** Give me your phone number.
815 Give me a chance.	**820** Give me a piece of that.
816 Give me a hint.	**821** Give me five more minutes.
817 Give me some water.	**822** Give me some space.
818 Give me some ideas.	

Study words & chunks!

⭐ Choose the correct words or chunks for each sentence and fill in the blanks. ▷

a hint

five more minutes

some water

some ideas

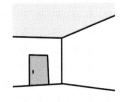

some space

a call

a chance

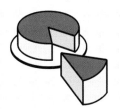

a piece of that

your phone number

814 Give me _____ . (전화)

815 Give me _____ . (기회)

816 Give me _____ . (힌트)

817 Give me _____ . (약간의 물)

818 Give me _____ . (몇몇 아이디어들[의견들])

819 Give me _____ . (너의 전화번호)

820 Give me _____ . (그것의 한 조각[부분])

821 Give me _____ . (5분 더)

822 Give me _____ . (약간의 공간)

Guess it!

⭐ In each picture, what would he or she most likely say?
Using '**Give me ~.**' make a sentence with the words or chunks below.

five more minutes	some space	a chance
a piece of that	some ideas	a call
your phone number	some water	a hint

1.

2.

3.

Speak Up!

⭐ Complete the dialogues with the best sentence from this track.

보기

> A: What time can we meet?
>
> B: Well, I'm not sure. **Give me your phone number**. I'll call you later.
>
> A: Okay. It's 010-2345-6789.

1

A: I think I like a boy in my class.

B: Who is it? 🎤 _____ ▷.

A: He is tall and has curly hair.

Ⓡ

2

A: Look at this little bird on the ground. It can't fly. I think it got hurt.

B: What can we do for it? 🎤 _____ ▷.

A: We should take it to my house. We can take care of it.

Ⓡ

3

A: We will play soccer after school. Do you want to join us?

B: I want to, but I have to stop by home first.

A: Alright. Then, 🎤 _____ ▷.

Ⓡ

세이펜을 통해 각 상황에 맞는 말을 직접 녹음해
보고 확실히 익혔는지 확인해보세요.

📖 [보기] sure 확실한 | later 나중에 **1.** curly hair 곱슬머리 **2.** get[got] hurt 다치다[다쳤다] | take A to B A를 B
로 데려가다 | take care of ~을 돌보다 **3.** want to ~하고 싶다 | have to ~해야 한다 | stop by ~에 잠시 들르다
| first 먼저 | then 그러면

93

Track

She gave me a smile.

그[그녀]는 나에게 ~을 줬어.

Say It! 다른 사람이 나에게 무엇을 주었는지 말할 때

Fill it! Listen to the track and fill in the blanks with the correct sentence number.

I.

A.

B.

H.

> **He[She] gave me ~.**

C.

G.

F.

E.

D.

823 She gave me a smile.

824 He gave me a tip.

825 He gave me some snacks.

826 She gave me a hug.

827 She gave me a birthday gift.

828 She gave me a lot of homework!

829 He gave me a different answer.

830 He gave me an allowance.

831 She gave me a warning.

Study words & chunks!

⭐ Choose the correct words or chunks for each sentence and fill in the blanks. ▷

a lot of homework

a warning

a tip

a different answer

some snacks

an allowance

a smile

a hug

a birthday gift

823 She gave me _____. (미소)

824 He gave me _____. (조언, 정보)

825 He gave me _____. (약간의 간식)

826 She gave me _____. (포옹)

827 She gave me _____. (생일 선물)

828 She gave me _____! (많은 숙제)

829 He gave me _____. (다른 대답)

830 He gave me _____. (용돈)

831 She gave me _____. (경고)

Guess it!

⭐ In each picture, what would he or she most likely say?
Using '**He[She] gave me ~.**' make a sentence with the words or chunks below.

a birthday gift	a smile	a lot of homework
a tip	an allowance	a different answer
some snacks	a hug	a warning

1. _____
_____.

2. _____
_____.

3. _____
_____.

Speak Up!

⭐ Complete the dialogues with the best sentence from this track.

> A: Why did that girl want to talk to you?
>
> B: You mean Jenny? **She gave me a birthday gift**. Yesterday was my birthday.
>
> A: Really? Happy late birthday!

1

A: How is your new English teacher?

B: He is nice. Now I can read words a lot better. 🎤 _____

_____ ▷ .

A: Really? What is it?   Ⓡ

2

A: I don't like my teacher much. 🎤 _____

_____ ▷ !

B: But didn't you say that she is the best teacher in the world?

A: Well, I take that back!   *I take that back! 그 말 취소야!   Ⓡ

3

A: The teacher said the answer was 20 for this problem.

B: Really? 🎤 _____ ▷ . He said 30 is correct.

A: Maybe we should ask him together.   Ⓡ

> 세이펜을 통해 각 상황에 맞는 말을 직접 녹음해 보고 확실히 익혔는지 확인해보세요.

📖 **[보기]** mean ~을 의미하다 | Jenny 제니(여자 이름) | really 정말 **1.** a lot 훨씬 | better 더 잘 **2.** best 최고의
3. say[said] 말하다[말했다] | correct 맞는, 정확한 | maybe 아마

94
Track

I'll show you my room.

내가 너에게 ~을 보여줄게(알려줄게).

Say It! 상대방에게 무언가 보여주거나 알려줄 때
*I'll은 I will을 줄인 말이에요.

Fill it! Listen to the track and fill in the blanks with the correct sentence number.

I. ___ A. ___ B. ___

H. ___

I'll show you ~.

C. ___

G. ___ F. ___ E. ___ D. ___

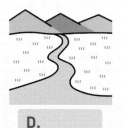

832 I'll show you my room.
833 I'll show you the way.
834 I'll show you my new phone.
835 I'll show you my favorite game.
836 I'll show you a picture of my sister.
837 I'll show you the difference!
838 I'll show you a shortcut.
839 I'll show you a magic trick.
840 I'll show you something interesting.

Study **words & chunks!**

⭐ Choose the correct words or chunks for each sentence and fill in the blanks. ▷

my new phone

a picture of my sister

my room

the way

something interesting

a shortcut

the difference

a magic trick

my favorite game

832 I'll show you _____. (내 방)

833 I'll show you _____. (길)

834 I'll show you _____. (나의 새 휴대폰)

835 I'll show you _____. (내가 가장 좋아하는 게임)

836 I'll show you _____. (내 여동생의 사진)

837 I'll show you _____! (다른 점)

838 I'll show you _____. (지름길)

839 I'll show you _____. (마술)

840 I'll show you _____. (무언가 재미있는 것)

Guess it!

⭐ In each picture, what would he or she most likely say?
Using '**I'll show you** ~.' make a sentence with the words or chunks below.

a magic trick	my new phone	a picture of my sister
the difference	the way	a shortcut
my favorite game	something interesting	my room

1. _____
_____ .

2. _____
_____ .

3. _____
_____ .

Speak Up!

⭐ Complete the dialogues with the best sentence from this track.

보기

A: **I'll show you something interesting**.

B: What is it?

A: It is a video clip of some animals. It's so funny.

1

A: I know how to go there. 🎤 _____ ▷.

B: Is it a shortcut?

A: Yes, it is. We can get there in five minutes! ⓡ

2

A: 🎤 _____ ▷.

B: Really? What is it?

A: I'll move a coin from your hand to mine. You won't see anything. ⓡ

3

A: Your dogs look the same. Which one is Max?

B: 🎤 _____ ▷! First, Max has a longer tail.

A: Oh, I see. And what else is different?　　*I see. 그렇구나. ⓡ

> 세이펜을 통해 각 상황에 맞는 말을 직접 녹음해 보고 확실히 익혔는지 확인해보세요.

📖 **[보기]** video clip 짧은 영상　**1.** how to ~하는 방법 | get 도착하다 | minute (시간) 분　**2.** really 정말 | mine 나의 것 | anything 아무것도　**3.** look ~해 보이다 | which 어느, 어떤 | longer 더 긴 | else 또 다른

95 Track

I'll tell you the truth.

내가 너에게 ~을 말해줄게(알려줄게).

Say It! 내가 상대방에게 무언가를 말해주거나 알려준다고 말할 때

Fill it! Listen to the track and fill in the blanks with the correct sentence number.

841 I'll tell you a story.	**846** I'll tell you one more thing.
842 I'll tell you a secret.	**847** I'll tell you something funny.
843 I'll tell you my plan.	**848** I'll tell you some surprising news.
844 I'll tell you the truth.	**849** I'll tell you my most embarrassing moment.
845 I'll tell you everything.	

Study words & chunks!

⭐ Choose the correct words or chunks for each sentence and fill in the blanks. ▷

one more thing

something funny

a secret

some surprising news

a story

everything

my plan

This is not real.

the truth

my most
embarrassing moment

841	I'll tell you _____ .	(이야기)
842	I'll tell you _____ .	(비밀)
843	I'll tell you _____ .	(내 계획)
844	I'll tell you _____ .	(사실, 진실)
845	I'll tell you _____ .	(모든 것)
846	I'll tell you _____ .	(한 가지 더)
847	I'll tell you _____ .	(무언가 웃긴 것)
848	I'll tell you _____ .	(놀랄만한 소식)
849	I'll tell you _____ .	(나의 가장 창피한 순간)

Guess it!

⭐ In each picture, what would he or she most likely say?
  Using '**I'll tell you** ~.' make a sentence with the words or chunks below.

the truth	everything	a secret
something funny	one more thing	a story
some surprising news	my most embarrassing moment	my plan

1. _____
   _____ .

2. _____
   _____ .

3. _____
   _____ .

Speak Up!

⭐ Complete the dialogues with the best sentence from this track.

> **보기**
>
> **A:** I can't guess what my gift is.
>
> **B:** Okay. **I'll tell you one more thing**. It's very small and round.
>
> **A:** Hmm... I still don't know.

1

A: 🎙 _____ ▶. But it might not work.

B: It's better than nothing. How can we surprise her?

A: Let's make a card. Everyone in class can write a message. Ⓡ

2

A: 🎙 _____ ▶.

B: Okay. What was that?

A: I was running to catch the bus, and my pants fell down! Ⓡ

3

A: 🎙 _____ ▶.

B: I'm not in the mood for jokes.

A: It will cheer you up a bit. Just listen. Ⓡ

> 세이펜을 통해 각 상황에 맞는 말을 직접 녹음해
> 보고 확실히 익혔는지 확인해보세요.

📖 **[보기]** round 둥근 | still 아직도　**1.** work (계획 등이) 잘되어 가다 | better than nothing 없는 것보다 나은 | surprise 놀라게 하다 | everyone 모든 사람 | message 메시지　**2.** fall[fell] down (옷이) 흘러내리다[흘러내렸다] **3.** in the mood for ~할 기분인 | joke 농담 | cheer A up A를 기운 나게 하다 | a bit 조금

96

Track

It makes me nervous.

그것은 나를 ~하게 만들어(그것 때문에 나는 ~해).

Say It! 무언가가 나를 어떤 기분이나 상태로 만든다고 말할 때

Fill it! Listen to the track and fill in the blanks with the correct sentence number.

I.

A.

B.

H.

It makes me ~.

C.

G.

F.

E.

D.

850 It makes me sad.

851 It makes me happy.

852 It makes me hungry.

853 It makes me angry.

854 It makes me sleepy.

855 It makes me proud.

856 It makes me excited.

857 It makes me nervous.

858 It makes me comfortable.

Study words & chunks!

⭐ Choose the correct words or chunks for each sentence and fill in the blanks. ▷

angry

proud

sad

hungry

happy

comfortable

excited

nervous

sleepy

850 It makes me _____. (슬픈)

851 It makes me _____. (행복한, 기쁜)

852 It makes me _____. (배고픈)

853 It makes me _____. (화난)

854 It makes me _____. (졸린)

855 It makes me _____. (자랑스러운)

856 It makes me _____. (신이 난, 들뜬)

857 It makes me _____. (긴장한)

858 It makes me _____. (편안한)

Guess it!

⭐ In each picture, what would he or she most likely say?
　　Using 'It makes me ~.' make a sentence with the words or chunks below.

happy	sad	nervous
sleepy	comfortable	angry
hungry	excited	proud

1. _____
　_____.

2. _____
　_____.

3. _____
　_____.

Speak Up!

⭐ Complete the dialogues with the best sentence from this track.

> 보기
>
> **A:** Mom is so angry. We are in big trouble.
>
> **B:** Stop biting your nails. **It makes me nervous**.

1

A: The book is so boring. 🎤 _____ ▷.

B: What is it about?

A: It is about a girl under some spell. It's the same old story. Ⓡ

2

A: I saw a picture of your brother on the wall. What did he do?

B: He won first place in a race. 🎤 _____ ▷.

A: That's cool. Ⓡ

3

A: He lost my pen again. This is the third time!

B: Again?

A: Yes! 🎤 _____ ▷. Ⓡ

> 세이펜을 통해 각 상황에 맞는 말을 직접 녹음해
> 보고 확실히 익혔는지 확인해보세요.

📖📖 **[보기]** in trouble 어려움에 처한 | nail 손톱　**1.** boring 지루한 | under a spell 주문[마법]에 걸려 있는 | some 어떤 | the same old story 뻔한 이야기　**2.** see[saw] 보다[봤다] | win[won] first place 일등을 하다[했다]　**3.** lose[lost] 잃어버리다[잃어버렸다] | third time 세 번째

97
Track

He made me do this.

그[그녀, 그것]는(은) 나를 ~하게 만들었어(했어).

Say It! 다른 사람이나 상황이 나를 어떻게 행동하게 했는지 말할 때

Fill it! Listen to the track and fill in the blanks with the correct sentence number.

I.

A.

B.

H.

He[She, It] made me ~.

C.

G.

F.

E.

D.

859 She made me cry.

860 He made me do this.

861 It made me feel sleepy.

862 It made me feel better.

863 She made me clean the room.

864 She made me study after dinner.

865 He made me wait for an hour!

866 She made me stay quiet.

867 It made me laugh out loud.

Study words & chunks!

⭐ Choose the correct words or chunks for each sentence and fill in the blanks. ▷

stay quiet

study after dinner

laugh out loud

do this

wait for an hour

cry

clean the room

feel better

feel sleepy

859 She made me _____. (울다)

860 He made me _____. (이것을 하다)

861 It made me _____. (졸리다)

862 It made me _____. (기분이 나아지다, 몸이 나아지다)

863 She made me _____. (방을 청소하다)

864 She made me _____. (저녁 식사 후에 공부하다)

865 He made me _____ ! (한 시간 동안 기다리다)

866 She made me _____. (조용히 있다)

867 It made me _____. (큰 소리로 웃다)

Guess it!

⭐ In each picture, what would he or she most likely say?
Using '**He[She, It] made me ~.**' make a sentence with the words or chunks below.

cry	laugh out loud	wait for an hour
study after dinner	clean the room	stay quiet
feel better	do this	feel sleepy

1.
_____

2.
_____

3.
_____

Speak Up!

⭐ Complete the dialogues with the best sentence from this track.

보기

> **A:** Why weren't you online last night?
>
> **B:** My mom didn't allow it. **She made me study after dinner**.

1

A: Did you have fun with Ben yesterday?

B: He was late yesterday. 🎤 _____ ▷!

A: Again? He really needs to change that habit.

Ⓡ

2

A: You must see that movie!

B: Why? Was it fun?

A: Definitely! 🎤 _____ ▷. It was

the best movie ever!   *Definitely! 물론!

Ⓡ

3

A: You looked so calm before the contest!

B: I listened to some music. 🎤 _____ ▷.

Ⓡ

세이펜을 통해 각 상황에 맞는 말을 직접 녹음해
보고 확실히 익혔는지 확인해보세요.

📖 **[보기]** online 온라인의 ㅣ allow 허락하다 **1.** have fun with ~와 재미있게 놀다 ㅣ Ben 벤(남자 이름) ㅣ really 정말
로 ㅣ need to ~해야 한다 **2.** best 최고의 ㅣ ever 지금까지 **3.** look[looked] ~해 보이다[보였다] ㅣ calm 침착한

98 Track

Let me tell you something.

내가 ～하게 해 줘. / 내가 ～해 줄게.

Say It! 1) 다른 사람에게 요청할 때
2) 다른 사람에게 도움을 제안할 때

Fill it! Listen to the track and fill in the blanks with the correct sentence number.

I.

A.

B.

Let me ~.

H.

C.

G.　F.　E.　D.

868	Let me know.	873	Let me think about it.
869	Let me try it.	874	Let me tell you something.
870	Let me go home.	875	Let me show you something.
871	Let me do it myself.	876	Let me ask you a question.
872	Let me use your pen.		

Study words & chunks!

ON OFF

⭐ Choose the correct words or chunks for each sentence and fill in the blanks. ▷

think about it

do it myself

ask you a question

tell you something

try it

know

go home

show you something

use your pen

868	Let me _____ .	(알다)
869	Let me _____ .	(그것을 해 보다)
870	Let me _____ .	(집에 가다)
871	Let me _____ .	(그것을 직접 하다)
872	Let me _____ .	(너의 펜을 사용하다)
873	Let me _____ .	(그것에 대해 생각하다)
874	Let me _____ .	(너에게 무언가를 말하다)
875	Let me _____ .	(너에게 무언가를 보여주다)
876	Let me _____ .	(너에게 질문을 하다)

Guess it!

⭐ In each picture, what would he or she most likely say?
   Using '**Let me ~.**' make a sentence with the words or chunks below.

think about it	tell you something	do it myself
try it	go home	show you something
ask you a question	use your pen	know

1. _____

2. _____

3. _____

Speak Up!

⭐ Complete the dialogues with the best sentence from this track.

> **A:** This science question is difficult. I don't know the answer.
>
> **B:** **Let me try it**. I'm good at science.
>
> **A:** Sure. I hope you can do it.   *Sure. 그래.

1

A: 🎤 _____ ▷. It's big news.

B: What is it?

A: Our teacher is getting married! I heard it from her.   ⓡ

2

A: Do you want to come over and play after school?

B: I don't know. 🎤 _____ ▷.

A: Okay.   ⓡ

3

A: 🎤 _____ ▷. What do you think of Jeff?

B: He's nice. But why do you ask?

A: I want him to join our club.   ⓡ

> 세이펜을 통해 각 상황에 맞는 말을 직접 녹음해 보고 확실히 익혔는지 확인해보세요.

📖 **[보기]** am[are, is] good at ~을 잘하다 **1.** get married 결혼하다 | hear[heard] 듣다[들었다] **3.** Jeff 제프(남자 이름) | want A to A가 ~하기를 원하다

Help me move the desk.

내가 ~하는 것 좀 도와줘.

Say It! 상대방에게 도움을 요청할 때

Fill it! Listen to the track and fill in the blanks with the correct sentence number.

A.

B.

C.

H.

Help me ~.

G.

D.

F.

E.

877 Help me find my notebook.	**881** Help me choose a present.
878 Help me move the desk.	**882** Help me think of an idea.
879 Help me open the bottle.	**883** Help me carry this box.
880 Help me clean the classroom.	**884** Help me solve the math problem.

Study words & chunks!

⭐ Choose the correct words or chunks for each sentence and fill in the blanks. ▷

open the bottle

choose a present

solve the math problem

clean the classroom

carry this box

move the desk

find my notebook

think of an idea

877 Help me _____. (내 공책을 찾다)

878 Help me _____. (책상을 옮기다)

879 Help me _____. (병을 열다)

880 Help me _____. (교실을 청소하다)

881 Help me _____. (선물을 고르다)

882 Help me _____. (아이디어를 생각해 내다)

883 Help me _____. (상자를 나르다)

884 Help me _____. (수학 문제를 풀다)

Guess it!

⭐ In each picture, what would he or she most likely say?
Using '**Help me ~.**' make a sentence with the words or chunks below.

find my notebook	clean the classroom	choose a present
carry this box	move the desk	think of an idea
	open the bottle	solve the math problem

1.

2.

3.

Speak Up!

⭐ Complete the dialogues with the best sentence from this track.

보기

A: Why are you still here? Let's go home!

B: Can you do me a favor? **Help me clean the classroom**.

A: Sure, I can help you.

*Can you do me a favor? 부탁 하나만 들어줄래?
*Sure. 물론이지.

1

A: 🎤 _____ ▷. I want to buy something

for my mom.

B: How about flowers?

Ⓡ

2

A: Are you busy now? 🎤 _____ ▷.

B: Okay. One, two, three! Oh, it's really heavy. What's inside?

A: These are all books.

Ⓡ

3

A: 🎤 _____ ▷. I can't get the right

answer.

B: Okay, let me see.

Ⓡ

세이펜을 통해 각 상황에 맞는 말을 직접 녹음해
보고 확실히 익혔는지 확인해보세요.

📖 **[보기]** still 아직도 | let's ~하자 **1.** something 무엇 | How about ~? ~은 어때? **2.** really 정말로 **3.** let me 내가 ~하게 해 줘

100
Track

I want you to believe me.

나는 네가 ~해주기를 원해(~해주면 좋겠어).

Say It! 상대방이 해주기를 원하는 일을 말할 때

Fill it! Listen to the track and fill in the blanks with the correct sentence number.

I.   A.   B.

I want you to ~.

H.   C.

G.   F.   E.   D.

885 I want you to ask him.

886 I want you to join us.

887 I want you to believe me.

888 I want you to listen to me.

889 I want you to think about it.

890 I want you to keep a secret.

891 I want you to come to my birthday party.

892 I want you to give it to him.

893 I want you to take a look at this.

Study words & chunks!

⭐ Choose the correct words or chunks for each sentence and fill in the blanks. ▶

keep a secret

ask him

listen to me

join us

give it to him

believe me

think about it

take a look at this

come to my
birthday party

885 I want you to _____. (그에게 묻다)

886 I want you to _____. (우리와 함께하다)

887 I want you to _____. (나를 믿다)

888 I want you to _____. (내 말을 듣다)

889 I want you to _____. (그것에 대해 생각하다)

890 I want you to _____. (비밀을 지키다)

891 I want you to _____. (내 생일파티에 오다)

892 I want you to _____. (그것을 그에게 주다)

893 I want you to _____. (이것을 보다)

Guess it!

⭐ In each picture, what would he or she most likely say?
Using '**I want you to ~.**' make a sentence with the words or chunks below.

come to my birthday party	join us	give it to him
listen to me	think about it	believe me
take a look at this	keep a secret	ask him

1. _____

2. _____

3. _____

Speak Up!

⭐ Complete the dialogues with the best sentence from this track.

> **보기**
>
> **A:** I didn't lie to you about anything. It's true.
>
> **B:** But you always say that.
>
> **A: I want you to believe me.**

1

A: Did you join a group yet? We need a good speaker like you.

B: Not yet.

A: Great! 🎤 _____ ▷ .

Ⓡ

2

A: 🎤 _____ ▷ .

B: What is it?

A: I don't know, but it looks like a small bug.

Ⓡ

3

A: Do you want to take swimming classes together?

B: Well... I don't know yet.

A: 🎤 _____ ▷ . It will be fun.

Ⓡ

> 세이펜을 통해 각 상황에 맞는 말을 직접 녹음해 보고 확실히 익혔는지 확인해보세요.

📖 **[보기]** anything 무엇, 아무것 **1.** yet 아직 | speaker 발표자 | like ～처럼 **2.** look like ～인 것처럼 보이다
3. want to ～하고 싶다 | take classes 수업을 받다 | swimming 수영

101
Track

I saw her talking to the teacher.

나는 그[그녀]가 ~하고 있는 것을 봤어.

Say It! 다른 사람이 어떤 행동을 하고 있는 것을 봤다고 얘기할 때

Fill it! Listen to the track and fill in the blanks with the correct sentence number.

I.

A.

B.

C.

H.

I saw him[her] -ing.

G.

F.

E.

D.

	894	I saw her crying.
895	I saw him sitting at his desk.
896	I saw her talking to the teacher.
897	I saw him playing basketball.
898	I saw her running to the bathroom.
899	I saw her entering the classroom.
900	I saw him crossing the street.
901	I saw her waving at someone.
902	I saw him getting scolded.

Study words & chunks!

⭐ Choose the correct words or chunks for each sentence and fill in the blanks. ▷

playing basketball

sitting at his desk

getting scolded

crossing the street

entering the classroom

running to the bathroom

talking to the teacher

waving at someone

crying

894 I saw her _____. (우는 것)

895 I saw him _____. (그의 책상에 앉아 있는 것)

896 I saw her _____. (선생님과 이야기하는 것)

897 I saw him _____. (농구하는 것)

898 I saw her _____. (화장실로 달려가는 것)

899 I saw her _____. (교실에 들어가는 것)

900 I saw him _____. (길을 건너는 것)

901 I saw her _____. (누군가에게 손을 흔드는 것)

902 I saw him _____. (야단맞는 것)

Guess it!

⭐ In each picture, what would he or she most likely say?
Using 'I saw him[her] -ing.' make a sentence with the words or chunks below.

crying	crossing the street	talking to the teacher
waving at someone	sitting at his desk	playing basketball
getting scolded	entering the classroom	running to the bathroom

1.

2.

3.

Speak Up!

⭐ Complete the dialogues with the best sentence from this track.

> **보기**
>
> **A:** Where is Mark? I don't see him.
>
> **B:** **I saw him playing basketball**. You can find him outside.

1

A: 🎤 _____ ▷.

B: Why? What happened to her?

A: She lost her dog.

ⓡ

2

A: 🎤 _____ ▷.

B: Why? Did he do something wrong?

A: The teacher said he cheated on the test.

ⓡ

3

A: Where's Jessica?

B: 🎤 _____ ▷.

A: Oh, I think she got carsick. I will go and check on her.

ⓡ

세이펜을 통해 각 상황에 맞는 말을 직접 녹음해
보고 확실히 익혔는지 확인해보세요.

📖 **[보기]** Mark 마크(남자 이름) ǀ outside 밖에서 **1.** happen[happened] (일이) 일어나다[일어났다] ǀ lose[lost] 잃어버리다[잃어버렸다] **2.** something 무엇 ǀ say[said] 말하다[말했다] ǀ cheat[cheated] 커닝하다[커닝했다] **3.** Jessica 제시카(여자 이름) ǀ get[got] carsick 차멀미하다[했다] ǀ check on 확인하다, 살펴보다

I heard him calling you.

102 Track

나는 그[그녀]가 ~하고 있는 것을 들었어.

Say It! 다른 사람이 어떤 행동을 하고 있는 것을 들었다고 말할 때

Fill it! Listen to the track and fill in the blanks with the correct sentence number.

I.

A.

B.

H.

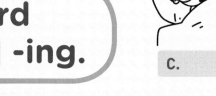

I heard him[her] -ing.

C.

G.

F.

E.

D.

903 I heard him singing.

904 I heard him calling you.

905 I heard her playing the piano.

906 I heard him talking about you.

907 I heard her talking on the phone.

908 I heard her laughing.

909 I heard him shouting.

910 I heard her complaining.

911 I heard him snoring.

Study words & chunks!

⭐ Choose the correct words or chunks for each sentence and fill in the blanks. ▷

playing the piano

singing

complaining

calling you

talking about you

snoring

shouting

talking on the phone

laughing

903 I heard him _____. (노래 부르는 것)

904 I heard him _____. (너를 부르는 것)

905 I heard her _____. (피아노를 연주하는 것)

906 I heard him _____. (너에 대해 얘기하는 것)

907 I heard her _____. (전화 통화하는 것)

908 I heard her _____. (웃는 것)

909 I heard him _____. (소리 지르는 것)

910 I heard her _____. (불평하는 것)

911 I heard him _____. (코를 고는 것)

Guess it!

⭐ In each picture, what would he or she most likely say?
   Using 'I **heard him[her] -ing.**' make a sentence with the words or chunks below.

playing the piano	complaining	snoring
laughing	calling you	singing
shouting	talking on the phone	talking about you

1.
_____
_____.

2.
_____
_____.

3.
_____
_____.

Speak Up!

⭐ Complete the dialogues with the best sentence from this track.

보기

A: Don't watch that movie.

B: Why? Was it bad?

A: Ellie was talking to her friends about it, and **I heard her complaining**.

1

A: 🎤 _____ ▷. Why is he in a good mood?

B: He's really excited about tomorrow.

A: Is it his birthday tomorrow? Ⓡ

2

A: Did something happen between you and him?

B: Not really. Why?

A: 🎤 _____ ▷. He sounded

a little bit upset. Ⓡ

3

A: He fell asleep during the class. 🎤 _____ ▷.

B: That's why he was in the teachers' room.

A: It was so loud. Everyone just laughed. Ⓡ

세이펜을 통해 각 상황에 맞는 말을 직접 녹음해 보고 확실히 익혔는지 확인해보세요.

📖 **[보기]** Ellie 엘리(여자 이름) **1.** in a good mood 기분이 좋은 | excited about ～ 때문에 신이 난 **2.** something 무엇 | happen (일이) 일어나다 | a little bit 조금 | upset 속상한 **3.** fall[fell] asleep 잠들다[잠들었다] | that's why 그래서 ～인 거야 | loud (소리가) 큰 | everyone 모든 사람

103

Track

I think (that) it's your turn.

나는 ~라고 생각해(~인 것 같아).

Say It! 내 의견을 표현하거나 내가 생각하는 것에 대해 말할 때
*말할 때는 that을 보통 빼고 말해요.

Fill it! Listen to the track and fill in the blanks with the correct sentence number.

MUSEUM

I.

A.

B.

C.

H.

I think (that) ~.

G.

F.

E.

D.

912 I think (that) you're right.

913 I think (that) it's your turn.

914 I think (that) I'm done.

915 I think (that) it's possible.

916 I think (that) I know the answer.

917 I think (that) it's going to rain.

918 I think (that) something is wrong.

919 I think (that) I left my bag behind.

920 I think (that) we should keep quiet.

Study words & chunks!

⭐ Choose the correct words or chunks for each sentence and fill in the blanks. ▷

we should keep quiet

I know the answer

you're right

something is wrong

it's your turn

I'm done

I left my bag behind

it's possible

it's going to rain

912 I think (that) _____ . (네가 옳다)

913 I think (that) _____ . (너의 차례이다)

914 I think (that) _____ . (나는 다 했다)

915 I think (that) _____ . (그것은 가능하다)

916 I think (that) _____ . (나는 답을 알다)

917 I think (that) _____ . (비가 올 것이다)

918 I think (that) _____ . (무언가가 잘못되다)

919 I think (that) _____ . (나는 내 가방을 두고 왔다)

920 I think (that) _____ . (우리는 조용히 해야 한다)

Guess it!

⭐ In each picture, what would he or she most likely say?
  Using '**I think (that)** ~.' make a sentence with the words or chunks below.

it's going to rain	I left my bag behind	something is wrong
I know the answer	you're right	I'm done
we should keep quiet	it's possible	it's your turn

1.
_____

2.
_____

3.
_____

Speak Up!

⭐ Complete the dialogues with the best sentence from this track.

A: <u>I think (that) it's going to rain</u>. It's getting darker.

B: You're right. Let's go inside! I don't want to get wet.

1

A: Do you think she likes me?

B: 🎤 _____ ▷. She gave you chocolate

last Valentine's Day.   Ⓡ

2

A: This sandwich tastes funny. How about yours?

B: 🎤 _____ ▷. Don't eat it.

You might get sick.   Ⓡ

3

A: 🎤 _____ ▷.

B: Already? That was fast.

A: I only had three questions to solve.   Ⓡ

세이펜을 통해 각 상황에 맞는 말을 직접 녹음해 보고 확실히 익혔는지 확인해보세요.

📖 **[보기]** darker 더 어두운 **1.** give[gave] 주다[주었다] | chocolate 초콜릿 | last 지난 | Valentine's Day 밸런타인데이 **2.** sandwich 샌드위치 | funny 이상한 | How about ~? ~은 어때? | yours 너의 것 | get sick 속이 안좋다 **3.** have[had] 가지다[가졌다] | solve 풀다

I don't think (that) it's true.

나는 ~라고 생각하지 않아(~인 것 같지 않아).

Say It! 내가 아니라고 생각하는 것에 대해 말할 때

Fill it! Listen to the track and fill in the blanks with the correct sentence number.

I.

A banana is yellow.

A.

B.

C.

H.

I don't think (that) ~.

G.

F.

E.

D.

921 I don't think (that) it's true.

922 I don't think (that) you did it.

923 I don't think (that) I can finish it.

924 I don't think (that) it's a good idea.

925 I don't think (that) I can join you.

926 I don't think (that) she lied to me.

927 I don't think (that) he is home now.

928 I don't think (that) I can make it.

929 I don't think (that) it really matters.

Study words & chunks!

⭐ Choose the correct words or chunks for each sentence and fill in the blanks. ▷

I can finish it

it's true

I can join you

he is home

it really matters

you did it

I can make it

it's a good idea

she lied to me

921 I don't think (that) _____. (그것은 사실이다)

922 I don't think (that) _____. (네가 그것을 했다)

923 I don't think (that) _____. (나는 그것을 끝낼[다 먹을] 수 있다)

924 I don't think (that) _____. (그것은 좋은 생각이다)

925 I don't think (that) _____. (나는 너희와 함께할 수 있다)

926 I don't think (that) _____. (그녀가 나에게 거짓말했다)

927 I don't think (that) _____ now. (그가 집에 있다)

928 I don't think (that) _____. (나는 해낼 수 있다)

929 I don't think (that) _____. (그것은 정말 중요하다)

Guess it!

⭐ In each picture, what would he or she most likely say?
Using '**I don't think (that) ~.**' make a sentence with the words or chunks below.

I can join you	I can finish it	it's true
you did it	I can make it	she lied to me
it really matters	he is home	it's a good idea

1. _____

_____ .

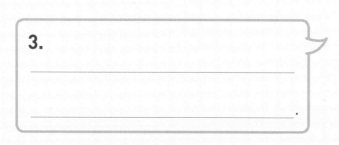

Mark's house

Mark

2. _____

_____ now.

3. _____

_____ .

Speak Up!

⭐ Complete the dialogues with the best sentence from this track.

> **보기**
>
> **A:** My phone is broken. Who did this? Did you see anything?
>
> **B:** No. Do you think it was me?
>
> **A:** No, **I don't think (that) you did it**.

1

A: We will go to an amusement park for a field trip!

B: 🎤 _____ ▷. My teacher said

we will go to a museum.

Ⓡ

2

A: Let's go out and play!

B: 🎤 _____ ▷. It's too hot today.

A: Okay. Then what should we do?

Ⓡ

3

A: Which color looks better on me? I can't decide.

B: 🎤 _____ ▷. Both of them

look good on you.

Ⓡ

세이펜을 통해 각 상황에 맞는 말을 직접 녹음해
보고 확실히 익혔는지 확인해보세요.

📖 **[보기]** broken 고장 난 | anything 무엇　**1.** amusement park 놀이공원 | field trip 현장 학습 | say[said] 말하
다[말했다]　**2.** let's ~하자　**3.** which 어떤 | look good[better] on ~에게 잘[더 잘] 어울리다

105
Track

I thought (that) it was over.

나는 ~라고 생각했어(~인 줄 알았어).

Say It! 과거에 내가 생각했던 일에 대해 말할 때

Fill it! Listen to the track and fill in the blanks with the correct sentence number.

I.

A.

B.

H.

I thought (that) ~.

C.

What's this?

G.

It wasn't me!

F.

E.

D.

930 I thought (that) it was you.

931 I thought (that) it was a lie.

932 I thought (that) it was over.

933 I thought (that) you liked it.

934 I thought (that) you knew.

935 I thought (that) you left already.

936 I thought (that) I had it in my bag.

937 I thought (that) you might say no.

938 I thought (that) you wanted to know.

Study words & chunks!

⭐ Choose the correct words or chunks for each sentence and fill in the blanks.

it was over

you left already

it was you

I had it in my bag

you liked it

you wanted to know

you knew

you might say no

it was a lie

930 I thought (that) _____. (그것은 너였다)

931 I thought (that) _____. (그것은 거짓말이었다)

932 I thought (that) _____. (그것은 끝났다)

933 I thought (that) _____. (너는 그것을 좋아했다)

934 I thought (that) _____. (너는 알았다)

935 I thought (that) _____. (너는 이미 떠났다)

936 I thought (that) _____. (나는 그것을 내 가방에 가지고 있었다)

937 I thought (that) _____. (너는 아니라고 말할지도 모른다)

938 I thought (that) _____. (너는 알고 싶어 했다)

Guess it!

⭐ In each picture, what would he or she most likely say?
Using 'I thought (that) ~.' make a sentence with the words or chunks below.

you left already	you knew	it was a lie
you wanted to know	it was over	you liked it
it was you	I had it in my bag	you might say no

1.
_____
_____ .

That's my sister!

2.
_____
_____ .

3.
_____
_____ .

Speak Up!

⭐ Complete the dialogues with the best sentence from this track.

> **보기**
>
> **A:** Why didn't you tell me before?
>
> **B:** I'm sorry. **I thought (that) you knew**. The teacher told us yesterday.

1

A: Why are you telling me this story?

B: 🎤 _____ ▷ .

A: Are you kidding? I asked about the homework.

*Are you kidding? 너 장난하니? Ⓡ

2

A: I don't want to eat that. It's too spicy for me.

B: 🎤 _____ ▷ . But there's no

other choice. Ⓡ

3

A: Didn't you hear? We don't have school tomorrow.

B: Really? 🎤 _____ ▷ .

A: No, it's true. The teacher told me. Ⓡ

세이펜을 통해 각 상황에 맞는 말을 직접 녹음해
보고 확실히 익혔는지 확인해보세요.

📖 **[보기]** tell[told] 말하다[말했다]   **2.** too 너무 | spicy 매운 | other (그 밖의) 다른 | choice 선택권   **3.** have
school 학교 수업이 있다 | really 정말

106
Track

I know (that) it's important.

나는 ~라는 것을 알아.

Say It! 내가 어떤 상황이나 사실에 대해 알고 있다고 말할 때

Fill it! Listen to the track and fill in the blanks with the correct sentence number.

I.

A.

B.

H.

I know (that) ~.

C.

G.

F.

E.

D.

939 I know (that) it's important.

940 I know (that) you are lying.

941 I know (that) I messed up.

942 I know (that) it's not your fault.

943 I know (that) it's embarrassing.

944 I know (that) I have to do it.

945 I know (that) you tried to help.

946 I know (that) you didn't mean it.

947 I know (that) you don't want to tell me.

Study words & chunks!

⭐ Choose the correct words or chunks for each sentence and fill in the blanks. ▷

you are lying

you tried to help

it's not your fault

I have to do it

it's important

you didn't mean it

you don't want to tell me

I messed up

it's embarrassing

939 I know (that) _____ . (그것은 중요하다)

940 I know (that) _____ . (너는 거짓말하고 있다)

941 I know (that) _____ . (나는 망쳤다)

942 I know (that) _____ . (그것은 네 잘못이 아니다)

943 I know (that) _____ . (그것은 창피하다)

944 I know (that) _____ . (나는 그것을 해야 한다)

945 I know (that) _____ . (너는 도와주려고 했다)

946 I know (that) _____ . (너는 그 뜻이 아니었다)

947 I know (that) _____ . (너는 나에게 말하고 싶지 않다)

Guess it!

⭐ In each picture, what would he or she most likely say?
Using '**I know (that)** ~.' make a sentence with the words or chunks below.

it's not your fault	you are lying	I have to do it
you don't want to tell me	it's embarrassing	it's important
you tried to help	I messed up	you didn't mean it

1.

_____

_____ .

I don't know what it is.

2.

_____

_____ .

3.

_____

_____ .

Speak Up!

⭐ Complete the dialogues with the best sentence from this track.

> **보기**
>
> **A:** I messed up everything. I'm so sorry.
>
> **B:** **I know (that) it's not your fault**. Stop blaming yourself.

1

A: I have to sing in front of the class. I don't think I can do it.

B: 🎤 _____ ▷. But you'll do fine. ⓡ

2

A: I didn't scribble in your textbook.

B: 🎤 _____ ▷. I saw everything.

A: Are you angry? It was all in good fun. I didn't mean to upset you. ⓡ

*It was all in good fun. 장난이었어.

3

A: You just stepped on my foot.

B: Oh, I am so sorry.

A: That's okay. 🎤 _____ ▷. ⓡ

세이펜을 통해 각 상황에 맞는 말을 직접 녹음해 보고 확실히 익혔는지 확인해보세요.

📖 **[보기]** stop -ing 그만 ~하다 | blame 탓하다 | yourself 너 자신 **1.** have to ~해야 한다 | in front of ~의 앞에 서 **2.** scribble 낙서하다 | see[saw] 보다[봤다] | everything 모든 것 | angry 화난 | mean to ~을 의도하다 | upset 속상하게 만들다 **3.** step[stepped] on 밟다[밟았다]

107

Track

I knew (that) it was you.

나는 ~이었다는 것을 알았어(알고 있었어).

Say It! 예전에 알고 있었던 일을 말할 때

Fill it! Listen to the track and fill in the blanks with the correct sentence number.

I.

This is a true story.
A.

B.

H.

I knew (that) ~.

C.

G.

F.

E.

D.

948 I knew (that) it was you.

949 I knew (that) it was mine.

950 I knew (that) you were there.

951 I knew (that) the story was true.

952 I knew (that) he was kidding.

953 I knew (that) it was your birthday.

954 I knew (that) something was wrong.

955 I knew (that) you could do it.

956 I knew (that) this would happen.

⭐ Choose the correct words or chunks for each sentence and fill in the blanks. ▶

something was wrong

it was mine

you could do it

this would happen

it was you

the story was true

it was your birthday

he was kidding

you were there

948 I knew (that) _____ . (그것은 너였다)

949 I knew (that) _____ . (그것은 내 것이었다)

950 I knew (that) _____ . (너는 그곳에 있었다)

951 I knew (that) _____ . (그 이야기는 사실이었다)

952 I knew (that) _____ . (그는 농담을 하고 있었다)

953 I knew (that) _____ . (너의 생일이었다)

954 I knew (that) _____ . (무언가가 잘못됐다)

955 I knew (that) _____ . (너는 그것을 할 수 있었다)

956 I knew (that) _____ . (이 일이 일어날 것이었다)

Guess it!

⭐ In each picture, what would he or she most likely say?
Using '**I knew (that) ~.**' make a sentence with the words or chunks below.

he was kidding	the story was true	this would happen
you were there	you could do it	something was wrong
it was your birthday	it was mine	it was you

1. _____

2. _____

3. _____

Speak Up!

⭐ Complete the dialogues with the best sentence from this track.

보기

> **A:** Congratulations! **I knew (that) you could do it**. You worked hard for it!
>
> *Congratulations! 축하해!
>
> **B:** Thank you. I tried my best, but I didn't expect it.

1

A: I drew something on the board. Did you see it?

B: 🎤 _____ ▷. It was really funny.

Ⓡ

2

A: He lied to me again! He's not going to move to another city.

B: Did you really believe that? 🎤 _____ ▷.

A: I thought it was true!

Ⓡ

3

A: Happy birthday! Here is your gift.

B: Did you remember my birthday? I'm so surprised. Thank you!

A: Sure. 🎤 _____ ▷. *Sure. 물론이지.

Ⓡ

> 세이펜을 통해 각 상황에 맞는 말을 직접 녹음해 보고 확실히 익혔는지 확인해보세요.

📖 **[보기]** work[worked] for ~을 위해 노력하다[노력했다] | hard 열심히 | try[tried] my best (내가) 최선을 다하다[다 했다] | expect 예상하다 **1.** draw[drew] 그리다[그렸다] | really 정말로 **2.** is[am, are] not going to ~하지 않 을 것이다 | move 이사하다 | think[thought] 생각하다[생각했다] **3.** surprised 놀란

I don't know what it means.

나는 ~이 뭔지 모르겠어.

Say It! 어떤 행동의 대상이 무엇인지 모르겠다고 말할 때

Fill it! Listen to the track and fill in the blanks with the correct sentence number.

I don't know what ~.

957 I don't know what you want.

958 I don't know what it means.

959 I don't know what I did wrong.

960 I don't know what I should do.

961 I don't know what you are talking about.

962 I don't know what I want to eat.

963 I don't know what I want to be yet.

964 I don't know what he is looking for.

965 I don't know what made you upset.

Study words & chunks!

⭐ Choose the correct words or chunks for each sentence and fill in the blanks. ▷

I did wrong

he is looking for

it means

made you upset

you want

I want to be

I want to eat

you are talking about

I should do

957 I don't know what _____ . (너는 ~을 원하다)

958 I don't know what _____ . (그것은 ~을 의미하다)

959 I don't know what _____ . (나는 ~을 잘못했다)

960 I don't know what _____ . (나는 ~을 해야 한다)

961 I don't know what _____ . (너는 ~에 대해 말하고 있다)

962 I don't know what _____ . (나는 ~을 먹고 싶다)

963 I don't know what _____ yet. (나는 ~이 되고 싶다)

964 I don't know what _____ . (그는 ~을 찾고 있다)

965 I don't know what _____ . (~이 너를 속상하게 만들었다)

Guess it!

⭐ In each picture, what would he or she most likely say?
  Using '**I don't know what ~.**' make a sentence with the words or chunks below.

it means	I want to eat	I did wrong
I want to be	I should do	you want
you are talking about	made you upset	he is looking for

1.

_____

_____ .

2.

_____

_____ yet.

3.

_____

_____ .

Speak Up!

⭐ Complete the dialogues with the best sentence from this track.

> **보기**
>
> **A:** <u>**I don't know what you want**</u>. You said no to everything.
>
> **B:** Sorry, I was being too picky. I'll make a decision now.

1

A: You look angry. Is something wrong?

B: No. I'm just in a bad mood.

A: 🎤 _____ ▷ . But cheer up!

*Cheer up! 힘내! Ⓡ

2

A: I missed this question. But 🎤 _____ ▷ .

B: Let me see. You didn't add 5 at the end.

Ⓡ

3

A: Do you know this word? 🎤 _____ ▷ .

B: It means "to decide what you are going to do." We learned it yesterday.

A: Did we? Let me check.

Ⓡ

> 세이펜을 통해 각 상황에 맞는 말을 직접 녹음해 보고 확실히 익혔는지 확인해보세요.

📖 **[보기]** say[said] 말하다[말했다] | everything 모든 것 | picky 까다로운 | make a decision 결정하다 **1.** look ∼해 보이다 | angry 화난 | something 무엇 | in a bad mood 기분이 안 좋은 **2.** miss 틀리다 | let me 내가 ∼하게 해 줘 **3.** are[am, is] going to ∼할 것이다

109 Track

I guess (that) you are right.

나는 ~이라고 추측해(~인 것 같아).

Say It! 내가 추측하거나 생각하는 것에 대해 말할 때

Fill it! Listen to the track and fill in the blanks with the correct sentence number.

I.

A.

B.

I guess (that) ~.

H.

C.

G.

F.

E.

D.

966 I guess (that) you are right.

967 I guess (that) I have no choice.

968 I guess (that) we're almost there.

969 I guess (that) it's broken.

970 I guess (that) I made a mistake.

971 I guess (that) I can get there in time.

972 I guess (that) he's not feeling good.

973 I guess (that) she doesn't want to do it.

974 I guess (that) we'll have to wait and see.

Study words & chunks!

⭐ Choose the correct words or chunks for each sentence and fill in the blanks. ▷

we're almost there

I made a mistake

I have no choice

I can get there in time

it's broken

he's not feeling good

you are right

she doesn't
want to do it

we'll have to
wait and see

966 I guess (that) _____ . (네가 옳다)

967 I guess (that) _____ . (나는 선택권이 없다)

968 I guess (that) _____ . (우리는 거의 도착하다)

969 I guess (that) _____ . (그것은 고장이 났다)

970 I guess (that) _____ . (나는 실수를 했다)

971 I guess (that) _____ . (나는 그곳에 제시간에 도착할 수 있다)

972 I guess (that) _____ . (그는 기분이 좋지 않다)

973 I guess (that) _____ . (그녀는 그것을 하고 싶지 않다)

974 I guess (that) _____ . (우리는 지켜봐야 할 것이다)

Guess it!

⭐ In each picture, what would he or she most likely say?
Using '**I guess (that)** ~.' make a sentence with the words or chunks below.

we're almost there	I made a mistake	she doesn't want to do it
I can get there in time	we'll have to wait and see	you are right
it's broken	he's not feeling good	I have no choice

1. _____ .

2. _____ .

3. _____ .

Speak Up!

⭐ Complete the dialogues with the best sentence from this track.

보기
> **A:** We are supposed to meet at five. Right?
>
> **B:** Yes. Why? Are you going to be late?
>
> **A:** No. **I guess (that) I can get there in time**.

1

A: 🎤 _____ ▷.

B: Why do you think so?

A: I heard her complaining about our group homework.

Ⓡ

2

A: Our team is losing. What a disappointment!

*What a disappointment! 정말 실망스럽다!

B: 🎤 _____ ▷.

They might do better at the end.

Ⓡ

3

A: There are only blue ones. I wanted to buy a green one.

B: But you need this.

A: You are right. 🎤 _____ ▷.

Ⓡ

세이펜을 통해 각 상황에 맞는 말을 직접 녹음해
보고 확실히 익혔는지 확인해보세요.

📖 **[보기]** are[am, is] supposed to ~하기로 되어 있다   **1.** so 그렇게 | hear[heard] 듣다[들었다] | complain 불
평하다   **2.** lose (경기, 시합에서) 지다 | do better 더 잘하다   **3.** there are ~이 있다 | want[wanted] to ~하
고 싶다[싶었다]

110 Track

I hope (that) you like this.

나는 ~하기를 바라(~하면 좋겠어).

Say It! 내가 바라는 것에 대해 말할 때

Fill it! Listen to the track and fill in the blanks with the correct sentence number.

I hope (that) ~.

I. A. B. H. C. G. F. E. D.

975 I hope (that) you like this.

976 I hope (that) our team wins.

977 I hope (that) the rain stops soon.

978 I hope (that) it works.

979 I hope (that) I can have a dog.

980 I hope (that) it's over soon.

981 I hope (that) we are in the same class.

982 I hope (that) you get better soon.

983 I hope (that) you don't mind.

Study words & chunks!

⭐ Choose the correct words or chunks for each sentence and fill in the blanks. ▷

the rain stops

it's over

I can have a dog

you get better

our team wins

it works

we are in the same class

you don't mind

you like this

975 I hope (that) _____. (너는 이것을 좋아하다)

976 I hope (that) _____. (우리 팀이 이기다)

977 I hope (that) _____ soon. (비가 그치다)

978 I hope (that) _____. (그것은 효과가 있다)

979 I hope (that) _____. (나는 개를 키울 수 있다)

980 I hope (that) _____ soon. (그것이 끝나다)

981 I hope (that) _____. (우리는 같은 반이다)

982 I hope (that) _____ soon. (너의 몸이 나아지다)

983 I hope (that) _____. (너는 신경 쓰지 않다)

Guess it!

⭐ In each picture, what would he or she most likely say?
Using '**I hope (that) ~.**' make a sentence with the words or chunks below.

it's over	you like this	it works
you get better	the rain stops	you don't mind
I can have a dog	our team wins	we are in the same class

1.

_____

_____ soon.

2.

_____

_____.

3.

_____

_____.

Speak Up!

⭐ Complete the dialogues with the best sentence from this track.

보기

A: Look! It started to rain!

B: Now we are in trouble. How can we go back home?

A: I know. **I hope (that) the rain stops** soon.

*I know. 맞아.

1

A: It's our last day of fourth grade.

B: Yes. I'm excited about having a new class.

A: 🎤 _____ ▷.

Ⓡ

2

A: 🎤 _____ ▷.

B: We will. We practiced very hard this time.

Ⓡ

3

A: How could you forget your password?

B: I am very forgetful these days. Hmm... Let me try this.

🎤 _____ ▷.

Ⓡ

세이펜을 통해 각 상황에 맞는 말을 직접 녹음해 보고 확실히 익혔는지 확인해보세요.

📖 **[보기]** in trouble 어려움에 빠진   **1.** fourth grade 4학년 │ excited about ~에 들뜬, 신이 난   **2.** practice [practiced] 연습하다[연습했다] │ this time 이번   **3.** password 비밀번호 │ forgetful 잘 잊어 버리는 │ these days 요즘

111
Track

I'm sure (that) it was a mistake.

나는 ~라고 확신해. / 분명히 ~할 거야.

Say It! 무언가가 확실하다고 말할 때

Fill it! Listen to the track and fill in the blanks with the correct sentence number.

I.

A.

B.

I'm sure (that) ~.

C.

H.

G.

F.

E.

D.

984 I'm sure (that) you'll like this.

985 I'm sure (that) you'll do fine.

986 I'm sure (that) we'll make it.

987 I'm sure (that) it was a mistake.

988 I'm sure (that) I said it.

989 I'm sure (that) I gave it back to you.

990 I'm sure (that) I put it on your desk.

991 I'm sure (that) there is a better way.

992 I'm sure (that) it's not going to be difficult.

Study words & chunks!

⭐ Choose the correct words or chunks for each sentence and fill in the blanks. ▷

I said it

you'll like this

there is a better way

it was a mistake

we'll make it

you'll do fine

I gave it back to you

it's not going to be difficult

I put it on your desk

984 I'm sure (that) _____. (너는 이것을 좋아할 것이다)

985 I'm sure (that) _____. (너는 잘할 것이다)

986 I'm sure (that) _____. (우리는 시간 맞춰 갈 것이다)

987 I'm sure (that) _____. (그것은 실수였다)

988 I'm sure (that) _____. (나는 그것을 말했다)

989 I'm sure (that) _____. (나는 그것을 너에게 돌려주었다)

990 I'm sure (that) _____. (나는 그것을 네 책상 위에 두었다)

991 I'm sure (that) _____. (더 나은 방법이 있다)

992 I'm sure (that) _____. (그것은 어렵지 않을 것이다)

Guess it!

⭐ In each picture, what would he or she most likely say?
Using '**I'm sure (that) ~.**' make a sentence with the words or chunks below.

you'll do fine	I said it	it's not going to be difficult
we'll make it	there is a better way	you'll like this
I put it on your desk	it was a mistake	I gave it back to you

1. _____ .

2. _____ .

3. _____ .

Speak Up!

⭐ Complete the dialogues with the best sentence from this track.

> **보기**
>
> **A:** Did you bring my pen?
>
> **B:** What are you talking about? **I'm sure (that) I gave it back to you**.
>
> **A:** No. I don't remember that at all.

1

A: I'm worried. I think we're going to be late.

B: Relax. _____ ▷. Ⓡ

2

A: Do you want to see something cool? _____

_____ ▷.

B: What is it?

A: But first close your eyes. Don't open them! Ⓡ

3

A: _____ ▷. Ⓡ

B: How can you be sure about that?

A: My teacher told me so. Don't worry.

세이펜을 통해 각 상황에 맞는 말을 직접 녹음해
보고 확실히 익혔는지 확인해보세요.

📖 **[보기]** not ~ at all 결코 ~하지 않는   **1.** worried 걱정하는 | are[am, is] going to ~할 것이다 | relax 진정하다
2. want to ~하고 싶다 | something 무엇 | cool 멋진 | first 먼저   **3.** tell[told] 말하다[말했다] | so 그렇게

Track 112

That's why I'm late.

그것이 ～한 이유야(그래서 ～인 거야).

Say It! 어떤 행동, 상황의 결과가 무엇인지 말할 때

Fill it! Listen to the track and fill in the blanks with the correct sentence number.

I.

A.

B.

That's why ~.

C.

H.

G.

F.

E.

D.

993 That's why I'm late.		**998** That's why I didn't tell you.
994 That's why I asked.		**999** That's why I'm not finished.
995 That's why I called you.		**1000** That's why it's so popular.
996 That's why she got angry.		**1001** That's why I changed my mind.
997 That's why I don't like it.		

Study words & chunks!

⭐ Choose the correct words or chunks for each sentence and fill in the blanks. ▶

I'm not finished

I'm late

I asked

I didn't tell you

I don't like it

she got angry

I called you

it's so popular

I changed my mind

993 That's why _____. (나는 늦었다)

994 That's why _____. (나는 물어봤다)

995 That's why _____. (나는 너에게 전화했다)

996 That's why _____. (그녀는 화가 났다)

997 That's why _____. (나는 그것을 좋아하지 않는다)

998 That's why _____. (나는 너에게 말하지 않았다)

999 That's why _____. (나는 끝마치지 못했다)

1000 That's why _____. (그것은 매우 인기 있다)

1001 That's why _____. (나는 내 생각을 바꾸었다)

Guess it!

⭐ In each picture, what would he or she most likely say?
Using '**That's why ~.**' make a sentence with the words or chunks below.

I didn't tell you	I don't like it	I called you
I'm late	it's so popular	I asked
she got angry	I'm not finished	I changed my mind

1. _____

2. _____

3. _____

Speak Up!

⭐ Complete the dialogues with the best sentence from this track.

> **보기**
>
> **A:** Are you going to buy this pencil case? I think Jane has the same one.
>
> **B:** I just realized that. **That's why I changed my mind**. I will get another one.

1

A: This jelly tastes too sour.

B: 🎤 _____ ▷. I really hate sour things. Ⓡ

2

A: The library got new comic books.

B: Really? Why didn't you tell me earlier?

A: 🎤 _____ ▷. But you didn't answer. Ⓡ

3

A: Look at that! There are so many people here.

B: I heard the juice is great here, and it's even cheap.
🎤 _____ ▷. Ⓡ

세이펜을 통해 각 상황에 맞는 말을 직접 녹음해 보고 확실히 익혔는지 확인해보세요.

📖 **[보기]** pencil case 필통 | Jane 제인(여자 이름) | realize[realized] 깨닫다[깨달았다] | get[got] 사다[샀다]; 얻다[얻었다] **1.** jelly 젤리 | really 정말 **2.** comic book 만화책 | earlier 더 일찍 **3.** there are ~이 있다 | hear[heard] 듣다[들었다] | juice 주스 | even 심지어

memo ✎

memo ✎

memo ✍

EGU
THE EASIEST GRAMMAR&USAGE

EGU 시리즈 소개

EGU
서술형 기초 세우기

영단어&품사

서술형·문법의 기초가 되는
영단어와 품사 결합 학습

문장 형식

기본 동사 32개를 활용한
문장 형식별 학습

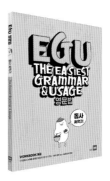

동사 써먹기

기본 동사 24개를 활용한
확장식 문장 쓰기 연습

EGU
서술형·문법 다지기

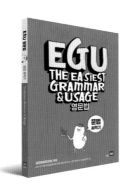

문법 써먹기

개정 교육 과정
중1 서술형·문법 완성

구문 써먹기

개정 교육 과정
중2, 중3 서술형·문법 완성

쎄듀북닷컴(www.cedubook.com)에서 부가 자료를 무료로 다운로드할 수 있습니다.

쎄듀

1 구문

판매 1위 '천일문' 콘텐츠를 활용하여 정확하고 다양한 구문 학습

(끊어읽기) (해석하기) (문장 구조 분석) (해설·해석 제공) (단어 스크램블링) (영작하기)

2 문법·서술형

쎄듀의 모든 문법 문항을 활용하여 내신까지 해결하는 정교한 문법 유형 제공

(객관식과 주관식의 결합) (문법 포인트별 학습) (보기를 활용한 집합 문항) (내신대비 서술형) (어법+서술형 문제)

3 어휘

초·중·고·공무원까지 방대한 어휘량을 제공하며 오프라인 TEST 인쇄도 가능

(영단어 카드 학습) (단어 ↔ 뜻 유형) (예문 활용 유형) (단어 매칭 게임)

4 선생님 보유 문항 이용

(Online Test) (OMR Test)

초 등 코 치

천일문
sentence

◆ ◆ ◆

WORKBOOK

with 세이펜

5

92 Track

Give me a hint.

나에게 ~을 줘.

Master words & chunks!

Ⓐ 상자 안에 있는 단어 조각들을 화살표로 연결하여 이번 트랙에서 배운 표현을 만들어 보세요.

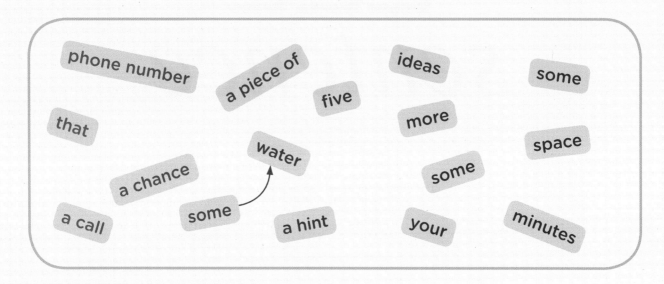

phone number · a piece of · ideas · some · that · five · more · space · water · a chance · some · a call · some · a hint · your · minutes

Ⓑ 상자에서 연결한 표현과 남는 단어 조각을 다시 한 번 써보고 뜻을 적어보세요.

Words & Chunks	뜻

Master sentences!

★ 앞에서 복습한 표현을 사용하여 이번 트랙에서 배운 문장을 각 그림에 맞게 완성해보세요.

나에게 ~을 줘.

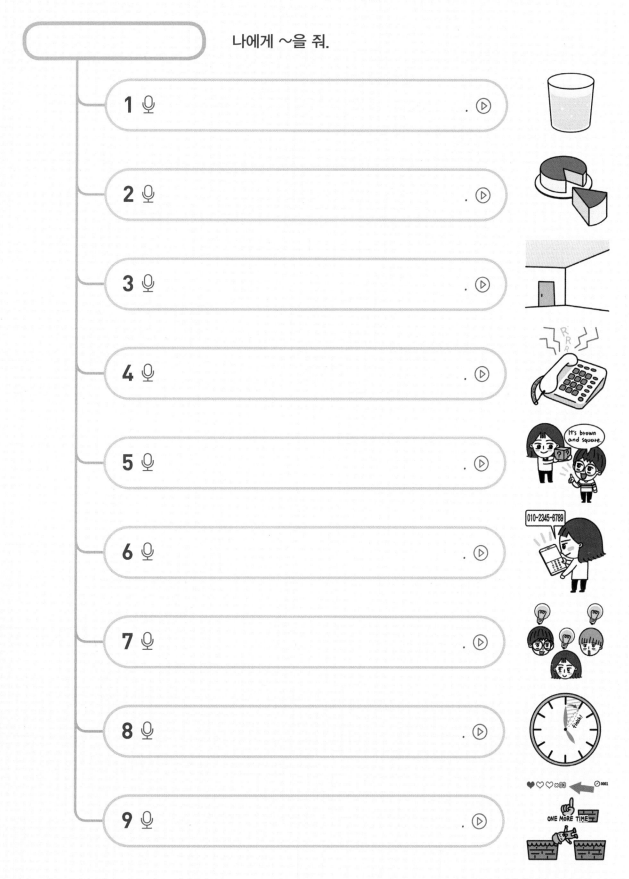

1 🎤 _____ . ▶

2 🎤 _____ . ▶

3 🎤 _____ . ▶

4 🎤 _____ . ▶

5 🎤 _____ . ▶

6 🎤 _____ . ▶

7 🎤 _____ . ▶

8 🎤 _____ . ▶

9 🎤 _____ . ▶

93 Track

She gave me a smile.

그[그녀]는 나에게 ~을 줬어.

Master words & chunks!

⭐ 아래 적혀 있는 한글 뜻에 알맞은 단어를 상자 안에서 찾아 완성하고, 주어진 영어 표현에는 알맞은 한글 뜻을 쓰세요.

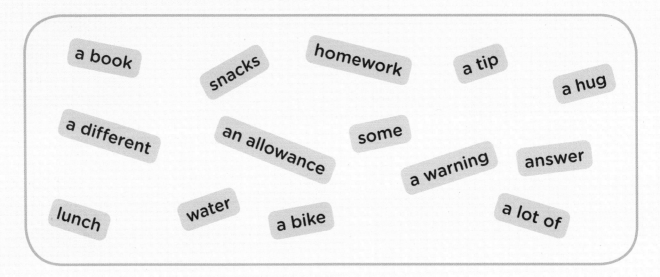

Words & Chunks	뜻
	많은 숙제
a smile	
	조언, 정보
a birthday gift	
	다른 대답
	포옹
	약간의 간식
	용돈
	경고

Master sentences!

★ 앞에서 복습한 표현을 사용하여 이번 트랙에서 배운 문장을 각 그림에 맞게 완성해보세요.

그는 나에게 ~을 줬어.

1 🎤 _____ . ▷

2 🎤 _____ . ▷

3 🎤 _____ . ▷

4 🎤 _____ . ▷

그녀는 나에게 ~을 줬어.

5 🎤 _____ . ▷

6 🎤 _____ . ▷

7 🎤 _____ ! ▷

8 🎤 _____ . ▷

9 🎤 _____ . ▷

I'll show you my room.

내가 너에게 ~을 보여줄게(알려줄게).

Master words & chunks!

Ⓐ 상자 안에 있는 단어 조각들을 화살표로 연결하여 이번 트랙에서 배운 표현을 만들어 보세요.

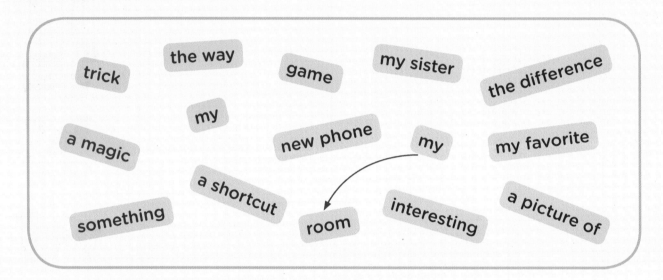

trick the way game my sister the difference

my my my favorite

a magic new phone

a shortcut

something room interesting a picture of

Ⓑ 상자에서 연결한 표현과 남는 단어 조각을 다시 한 번 써보고 뜻을 적어보세요.

Words & Chunks	뜻

Master sentences!

★ 앞에서 복습한 표현을 사용하여 이번 트랙에서 배운 문장을 각 그림에 맞게 완성해보세요.

[ ] 내가 너에게 ~을 보여줄게(알려줄게).

1 ____________________ .

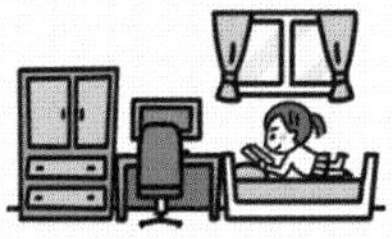

2 ____________________ .

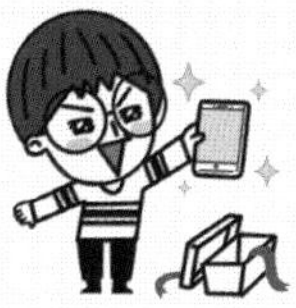

3 ____________________ .

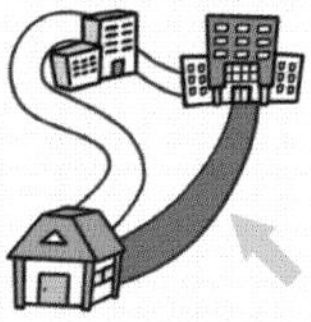

4 ____________________ .

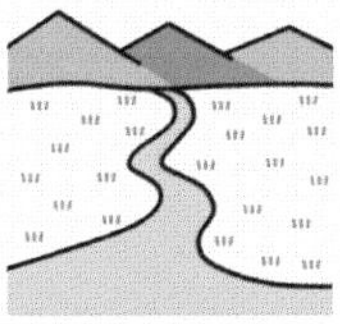

5 ____________________ !

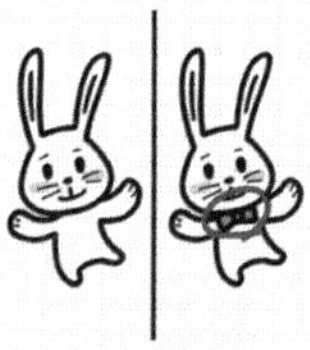

6 ____________________ .

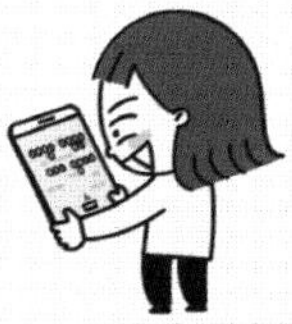

7 ____________________ .

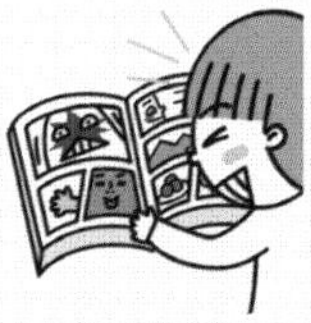

8 ____________________ .

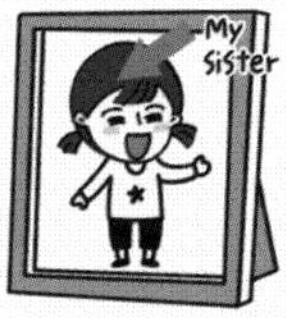

9 ____________________ .

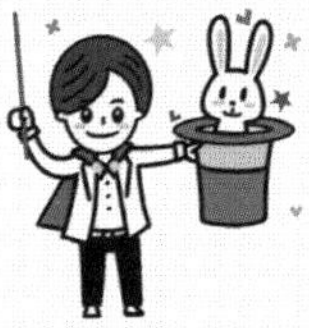

95
Track

I'll tell you the truth.

내가 너에게 ~을 말해줄게(알려줄게).

Master words & chunks!

⭐ 아래 적혀 있는 한글 뜻에 알맞은 단어를 상자 안에서 찾아 완성하고, 주어진 영어 표현에는 알맞은 한글 뜻을 쓰세요.

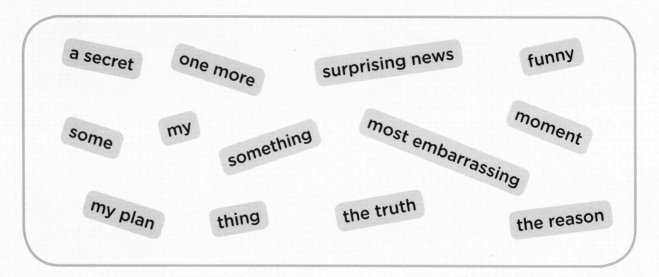

a secret   one more   surprising news   funny

some   my   something   most embarrassing   moment

my plan   thing   the truth   the reason

Words & Chunks	뜻
	비밀
	내 계획
	무언가 웃긴 것
	사실, 진실
	놀랄만한 소식
	나의 가장 창피한 순간
a story	
everything	
	한 가지 더

Master sentences!

⭐ 앞에서 복습한 표현을 사용하여 이번 트랙에서 배운 문장을 각 그림에 맞게 완성해보세요.

내가 너에게 ~을 말해줄게(알려줄게).

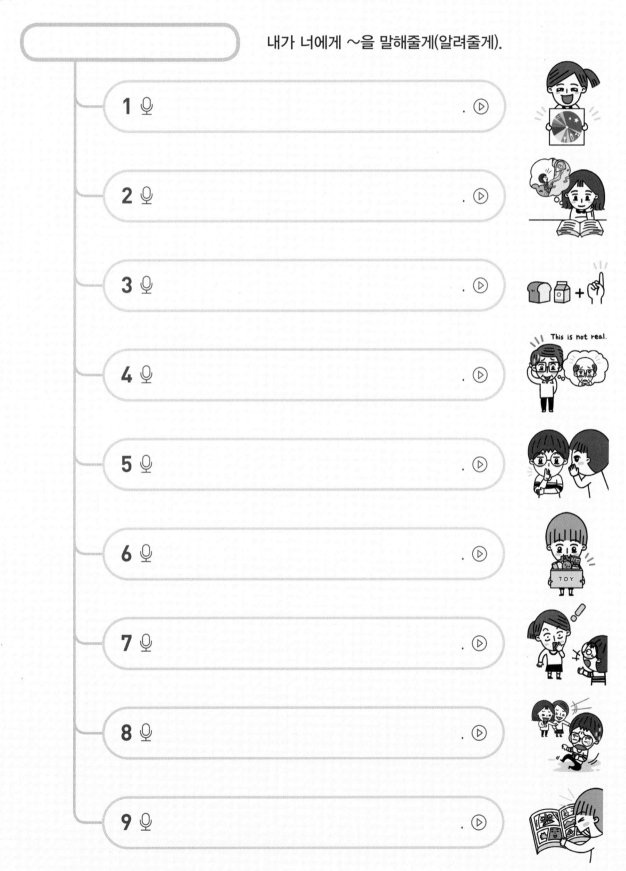

96
Track

It makes me nervous.

그것은 나를 ~하게 만들어(그것 때문에 나는 ~해).

Master words & chunks!

⭐ 아래 적혀 있는 한글 뜻에 알맞은 단어를 상자 안에서 찾아 완성하고, 주어진 영어 표현에는 알맞은 한글 뜻을 쓰세요.

sleepy   comfortable   excited   busy

sick   calm   happy   bad   angry

sad   hungry   scared

Words & Chunks	뜻
	슬픈
	신이 난, 들뜬
nervous	
	화난
	행복한, 기쁜
	편안한
	졸린
proud	
	배고픈

Master sentences!

★ 앞에서 복습한 표현을 사용하여 이번 트랙에서 배운 문장을 각 그림에 맞게 완성해보세요.

그것은 나를 ~하게 만들어.
(그것 때문에 나는 ~해.)

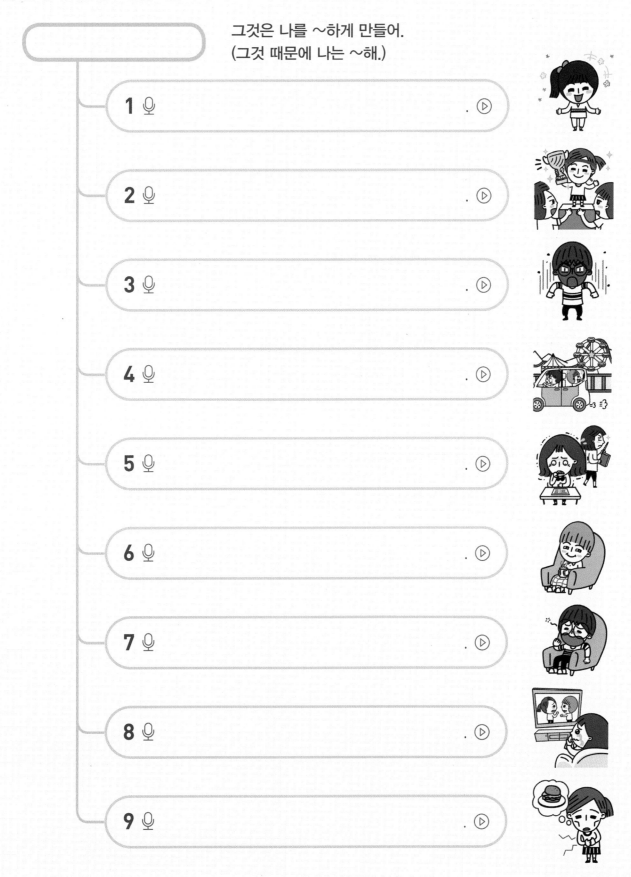

1 🎤 .

2 🎤 .

3 🎤 .

4 🎤 .

5 🎤 .

6 🎤 .

7 🎤 .

8 🎤 .

9 🎤 .

97 Track

He made me do this.

그[그녀, 그것]는(은) 나를 ~하게 만들었어(했어).

Master words & chunks!

Ⓐ 상자 안에 있는 단어 조각들을 화살표로 연결하여 이번 트랙에서 배운 표현을 만들어 보세요.

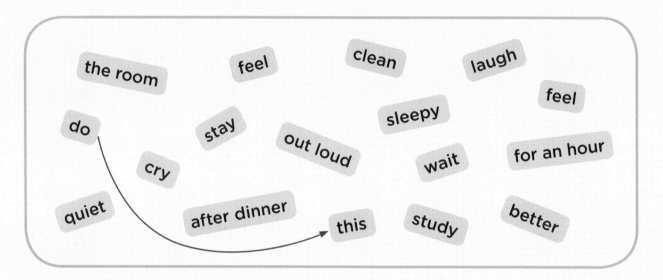

Ⓑ 상자에서 연결한 표현과 남는 단어 조각을 다시 한 번 써보고 뜻을 적어보세요.

Words & Chunks	뜻

Master sentences!

⭐ 앞에서 복습한 표현을 사용하여 이번 트랙에서 배운 문장을 각 그림에 맞게 완성해보세요.

그는 나를 ～하게 만들었어(했어).

1 🎤   ! ▶

2 🎤   . ▶

3 🎤   . ▶

그녀는 나를 ～하게 만들었어(했어).

4 🎤   . ▶

5 🎤   . ▶

6 🎤   . ▶

7 🎤   . ▶

그것은 나를 ～하게 만들었어(했어).

8 🎤   . ▶

9 🎤   . ▶

98
Track

Let me tell you something.

내가 ~하게 해 줘. / 내가 ~해 줄게.

Master words & chunks!

Ⓐ 상자 안에 있는 단어 조각들을 화살표로 연결하여 이번 트랙에서 배운 표현을 만들어 보세요.

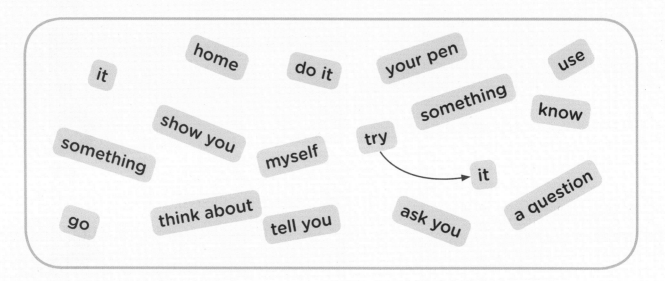

Ⓑ 상자에서 연결한 표현과 남는 단어 조각을 다시 한 번 써보고 뜻을 적어보세요.

Words & Chunks	뜻

Master sentences!

★ 앞에서 복습한 표현을 사용하여 이번 트랙에서 배운 문장을 각 그림에 맞게 완성해보세요.

내가 ~하게 해 줘. / 내가 ~해 줄게.

1 🎤 _____ . ▷

2 🎤 _____ . ▷

3 🎤 _____ . ▷

4 🎤 _____ . ▷

5 🎤 _____ . ▷

6 🎤 _____ . ▷

7 🎤 _____ . ▷

8 🎤 _____ . ▷

9 🎤 _____ . ▷

99
Track

Help me move the desk.

내가 ~하는 것 좀 도와줘.

Master words & chunks!

Ⓐ 상자 안에 있는 단어 조각들을 화살표로 연결하여 이번 트랙에서 배운 표현을 만들어 보세요.

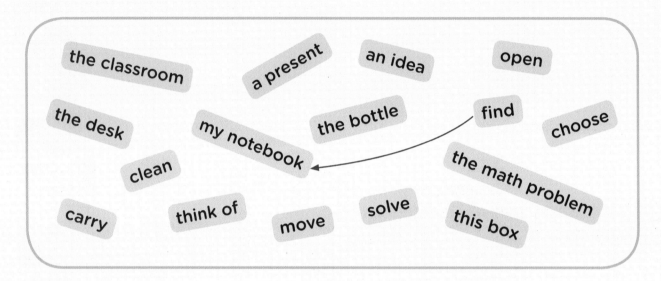

Ⓑ 상자에서 연결한 표현을 다시 한 번 써보고 뜻을 적어보세요.

Words & Chunks	뜻

Master sentences!

★ 앞에서 복습한 표현을 사용하여 이번 트랙에서 배운 문장을 각 그림에 맞게 완성해보세요.

내가 ~하는 것 좀 도와줘.

100
Track

I want you to believe me.

나는 네가 ~해주기를 원해(~해주면 좋겠어).

Master words & chunks!

Ⓐ 상자 안에 있는 단어 조각들을 화살표로 연결하여 이번 트랙에서 배운 표현을 만들어 보세요.

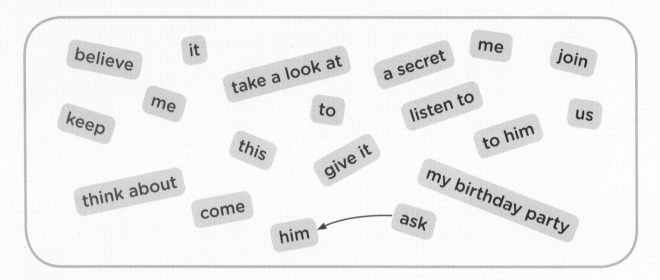

Ⓑ 상자에서 연결한 표현을 다시 한 번 써보고 뜻을 적어보세요.

Words & Chunks	뜻

Master sentences!

⭐ 앞에서 복습한 표현을 사용하여 이번 트랙에서 배운 문장을 각 그림에 맞게 완성해보세요.

나는 네가 ~해주기를 원해(~해주면 좋겠어).

101 Track

I saw her talking to the teacher.

나는 그[그녀]가 ~하고 있는 것을 봤어.

Master words & chunks!

Ⓐ 상자 안에 있는 단어 조각들을 화살표로 연결하여 이번 트랙에서 배운 표현을 만들어 보세요.

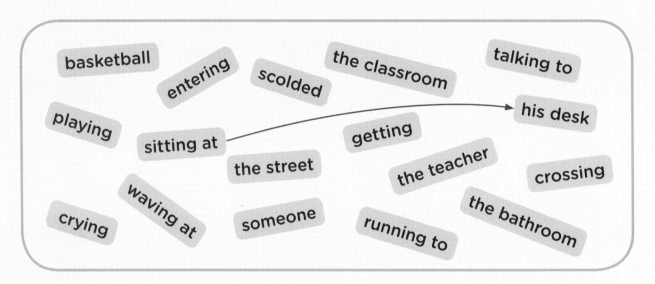

Ⓑ 상자에서 연결한 표현과 남는 단어 조각을 다시 한 번 써보고 뜻을 적어보세요.

Words & Chunks	뜻

Master sentences!

앞에서 복습한 표현을 사용하여 이번 트랙에서 배운 문장을 각 그림에 맞게 완성해보세요.

나는 그가 ~하고 있는 것을 봤어.

1

2

3

4

나는 그녀가 ~하고 있는 것을 봤어.

5

6

7

8

9

102 Track

I heard him calling you.

나는 그[그녀]가 ~하고 있는 것을 들었어.

Master words & chunks!

⭐ 아래 적혀 있는 한글 뜻에 알맞은 단어를 상자 안에서 찾아 완성하고, 주어진 영어 표현에는 알맞은 한글 뜻을 쓰세요.

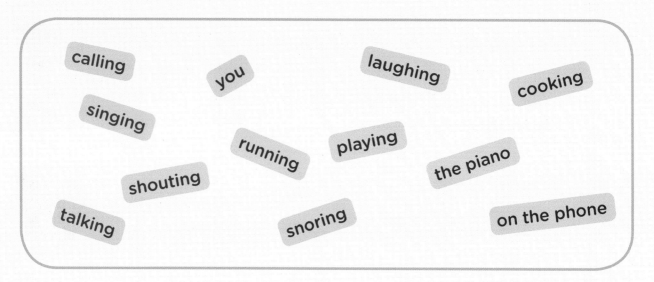

Words & Chunks	뜻
	웃는 것
talking about you	
	코를 고는 것
	노래 부르는 것
	너를 부르는 것
	피아노를 연주하는 것
	소리 지르는 것
complaining	
	전화 통화하는 것

Master sentences!

★ 앞에서 복습한 표현을 사용하여 이번 트랙에서 배운 문장을 각 그림에 맞게 완성해보세요.

나는 그가 ～하고 있는 것을 들었어.

1 🎤 _____ . ▷

2 🎤 _____ . ▷

3 🎤 _____ . ▷

4 🎤 _____ . ▷

5 🎤 _____ . ▷

나는 그녀가 ～하고 있는 것을 들었어.

6 🎤 _____ . ▷

7 🎤 _____ . ▷

8 🎤 _____ . ▷

9 🎤 _____ . ▷

103
Track

I think (that) it's your turn.

나는 ～라고 생각해(～인 것 같아).

Master words & chunks!

Ⓐ 상자 안에 있는 단어 조각들을 화살표로 연결하여 이번 트랙에서 배운 표현을 만들어 보세요.

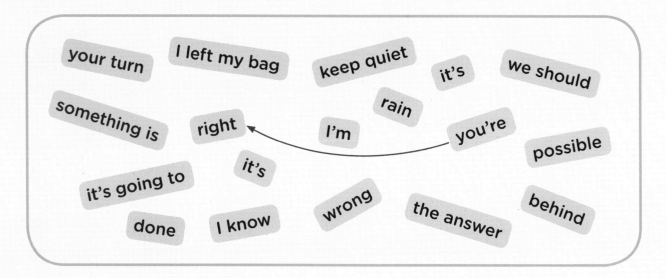

Ⓑ 상자에서 연결한 표현을 다시 한 번 써보고 뜻을 적어보세요.

Words & Chunks	뜻

Master sentences!

⭐ 앞에서 복습한 표현을 사용하여 이번 트랙에서 배운 문장을 각 그림에 맞게 완성해보세요.

나는 ～라고 생각해(～인 것 같아).

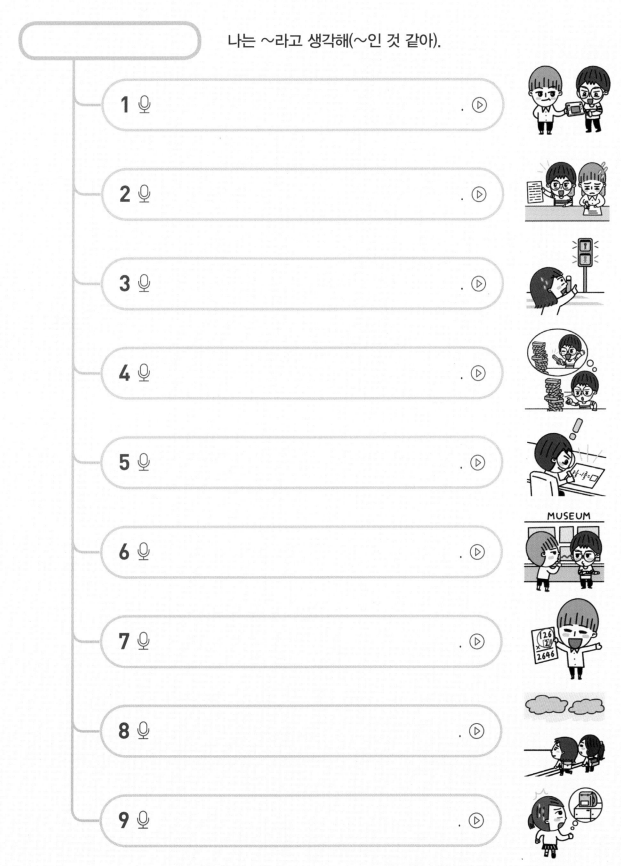

1 🎤 ▷

2 🎤 ▷

3 🎤 ▷

4 🎤 ▷

5 🎤 ▷

6 🎤 ▷

7 🎤 ▷

8 🎤 ▷

9 🎤 ▷

I don't think (that) it's true.

나는 ~라고 생각하지 않아(~인 것 같지 않아).

Master words & chunks!

Ⓐ 상자 안에 있는 단어 조각들을 화살표로 연결하여 이번 트랙에서 배운 표현을 만들어 보세요.

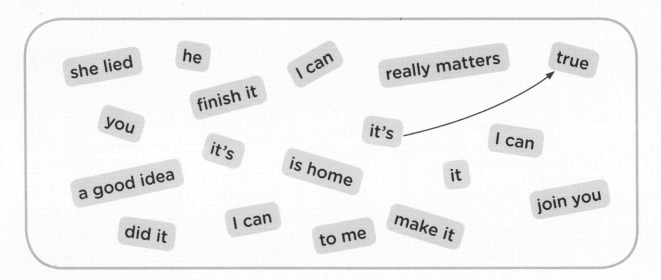

Ⓑ 상자에서 연결한 표현과 남는 단어 조각을 다시 한 번 써보고 뜻을 적어보세요.

Words & Chunks	뜻

Master sentences!

⭐ 앞에서 복습한 표현을 사용하여 이번 트랙에서 배운 문장을 각 그림에 맞게 완성해보세요.

나는 ~라고 생각하지 않아(~인 것 같지 않아).

1 🎤 _____ . ▷

2 🎤 _____ . ▷

3 🎤 _____ . ▷

4 🎤 _____ now. ▷

5 🎤 _____ . ▷

6 🎤 _____ . ▷

7 🎤 _____ . ▷

8 🎤 _____ . ▷

9 🎤 _____ . ▷

105

Track

I thought (that) it was over.

나는 ~라고 생각했어(~인 줄 알았어).

Master words & chunks!

(A) 상자 안에 있는 단어 조각들을 화살표로 연결하여 이번 트랙에서 배운 표현을 만들어 보세요.

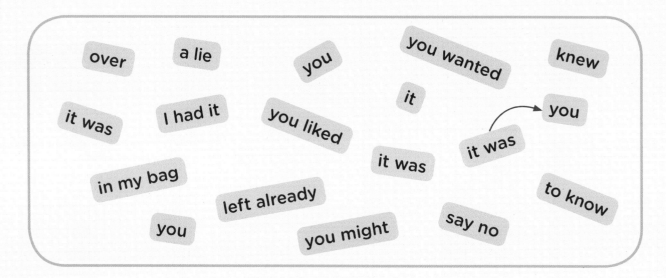

(B) 상자에서 연결한 표현을 다시 한 번 써보고 뜻을 적어보세요.

Words & Chunks	뜻

Master sentences!

⭐ 앞에서 복습한 표현을 사용하여 이번 트랙에서 배운 문장을 각 그림에 맞게 완성해보세요.

나는 ~라고 생각했어(~인 줄 알았어).

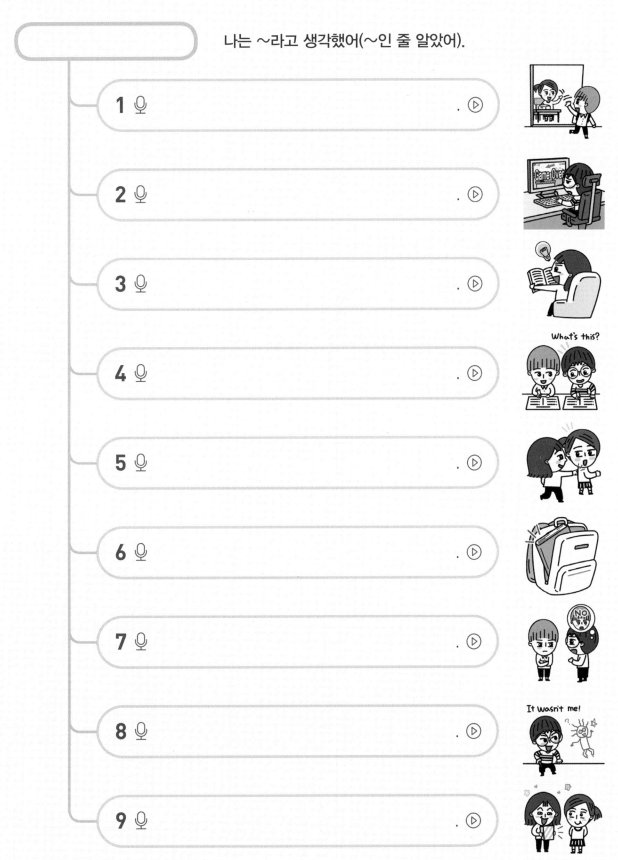

1 🎤 　　　　　　　　　　　　　　　　　　. ▷

2 🎤 　　　　　　　　　　　　　　　　　　. ▷

3 🎤 　　　　　　　　　　　　　　　　　　. ▷

4 🎤 　　　　　　　　　　　　　　　　　　. ▷

5 🎤 　　　　　　　　　　　　　　　　　　. ▷

6 🎤 　　　　　　　　　　　　　　　　　　. ▷

7 🎤 　　　　　　　　　　　　　　　　　　. ▷

8 🎤 　　　　　　　　　　　　　　　　　　. ▷

9 🎤 　　　　　　　　　　　　　　　　　　. ▷

106 Track

I know (that) it's important.

나는 ~라는 것을 알아.

Master words & chunks!

Ⓐ 상자 안에 있는 단어 조각들을 화살표로 연결하여 이번 트랙에서 배운 표현을 만들어 보세요.

Ⓑ 상자에서 연결한 표현을 다시 한 번 써보고 뜻을 적어보세요.

Words & Chunks	뜻

Master sentences!

⭐ 앞에서 복습한 표현을 사용하여 이번 트랙에서 배운 문장을 각 그림에 맞게 완성해보세요.

나는 ~라는 것을 알아.

1 🎤 _____ . ▷

2 🎤 _____ . ▷

3 🎤 _____ . ▷

4 🎤 _____ . ▷

5 🎤 _____ . ▷

6 🎤 _____ . ▷

7 🎤 _____ . ▷

8 🎤 _____ . ▷

9 🎤 _____ . ▷

107
Track

I knew (that) it was you.

나는 ~이었다는 것을 알았어(알고 있었어).

Master words & chunks!

Ⓐ 상자 안에 있는 단어 조각들을 화살표로 연결하여 이번 트랙에서 배운 표현을 만들어 보세요.

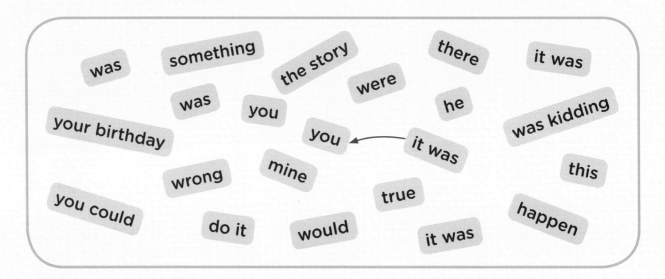

Ⓑ 상자에서 연결한 표현을 다시 한 번 써보고 뜻을 적어보세요.

Words & Chunks	뜻

Master sentences!

★ 앞에서 복습한 표현을 사용하여 이번 트랙에서 배운 문장을 각 그림에 맞게 완성해보세요.

나는 ~이었다는 것을 알았어(알고 있었어).

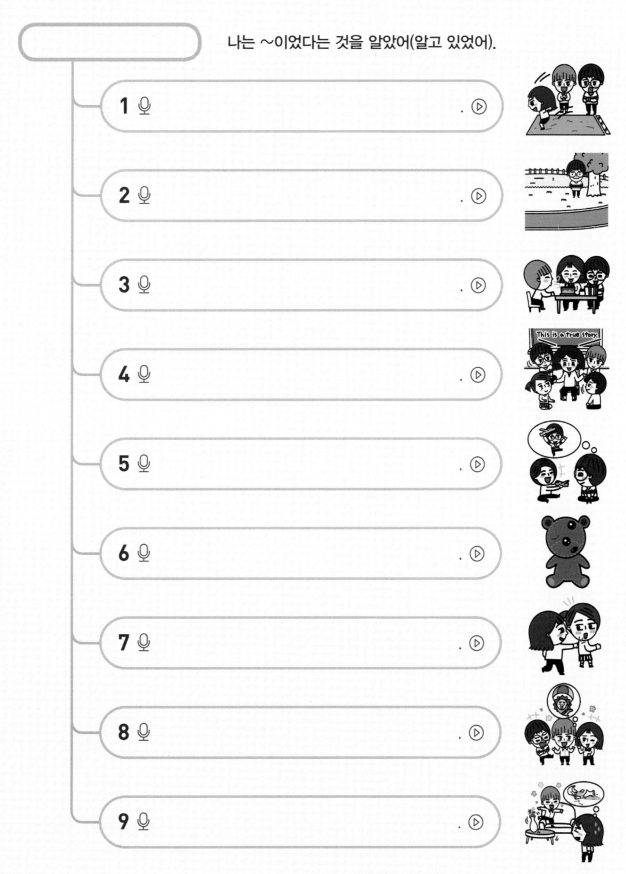

1 🎤 _____ . ▷

2 🎤 _____ . ▷

3 🎤 _____ . ▷

4 🎤 _____ . ▷

5 🎤 _____ . ▷

6 🎤 _____ . ▷

7 🎤 _____ . ▷

8 🎤 _____ . ▷

9 🎤 _____ . ▷

108
Track

I don't know what it means.

나는 ~이 뭔지 모르겠어.

Master words & chunks!

Ⓐ 상자 안에 있는 단어 조각들을 화살표로 연결하여 이번 트랙에서 배운 표현을 만들어 보세요.

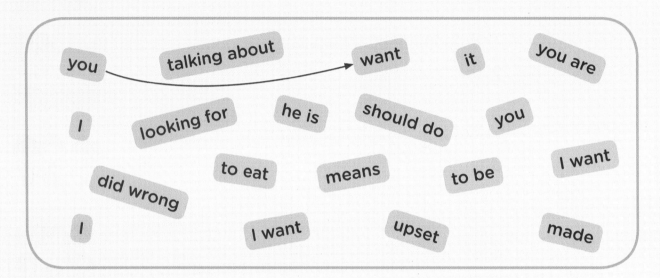

Ⓑ 상자에서 연결한 표현을 다시 한 번 써보고 뜻을 적어보세요.

Words & Chunks	뜻

Master sentences!

⭐ 앞에서 복습한 표현을 사용하여 이번 트랙에서 배운 문장을 각 그림에 맞게 완성해보세요.

나는 ~이 뭔지 모르겠어.

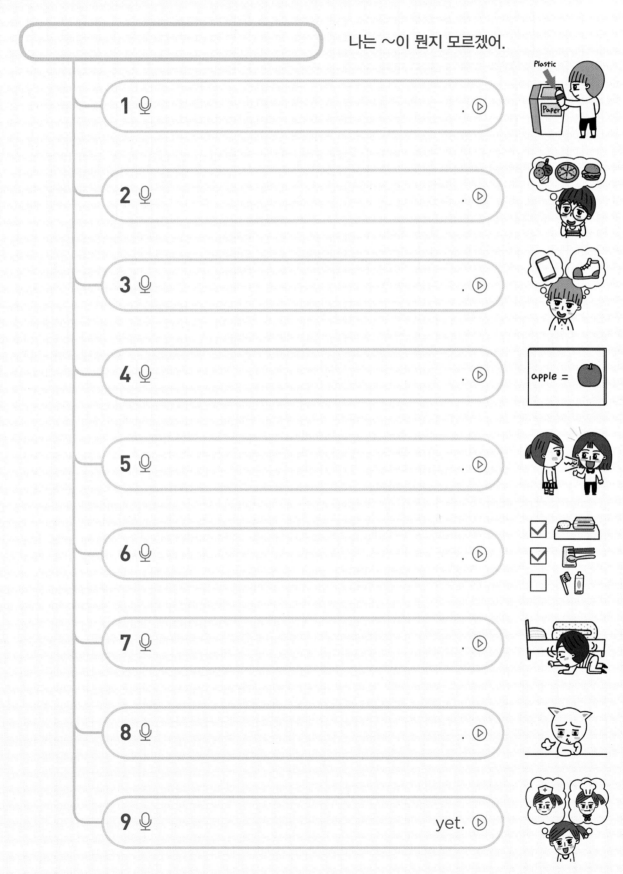

1 🎤 _____ . ▷

2 🎤 _____ . ▷

3 🎤 _____ . ▷

4 🎤 _____ . ▷

5 🎤 _____ . ▷

6 🎤 _____ . ▷

7 🎤 _____ . ▷

8 🎤 _____ . ▷

9 🎤 _____ yet. ▷

109
Track

I guess (that) you are right.

나는 ~라고 추측해(~인 것 같아).

Master words & chunks!

Ⓐ 상자 안에 있는 단어 조각들을 화살표로 연결하여 이번 트랙에서 배운 표현을 만들어 보세요.

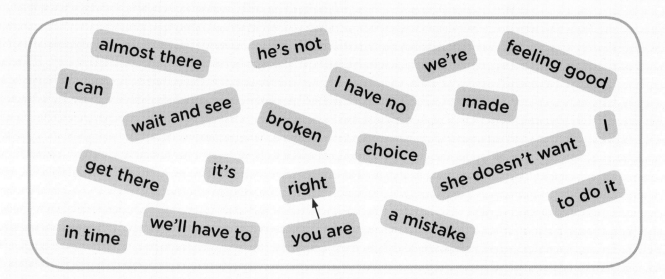

almost there
he's not
we're
feeling good
I can
I have no
made
wait and see
broken
choice
I
get there
it's
she doesn't want
right
to do it
in time
we'll have to
you are
a mistake

Ⓑ 상자에서 연결한 표현을 다시 한 번 써보고 뜻을 적어보세요.

Words & Chunks	뜻

Master sentences!

⭐ 앞에서 복습한 표현을 사용하여 이번 트랙에서 배운 문장을 각 그림에 맞게 완성해보세요.

나는 ~라고 추측해(~인 것 같아).

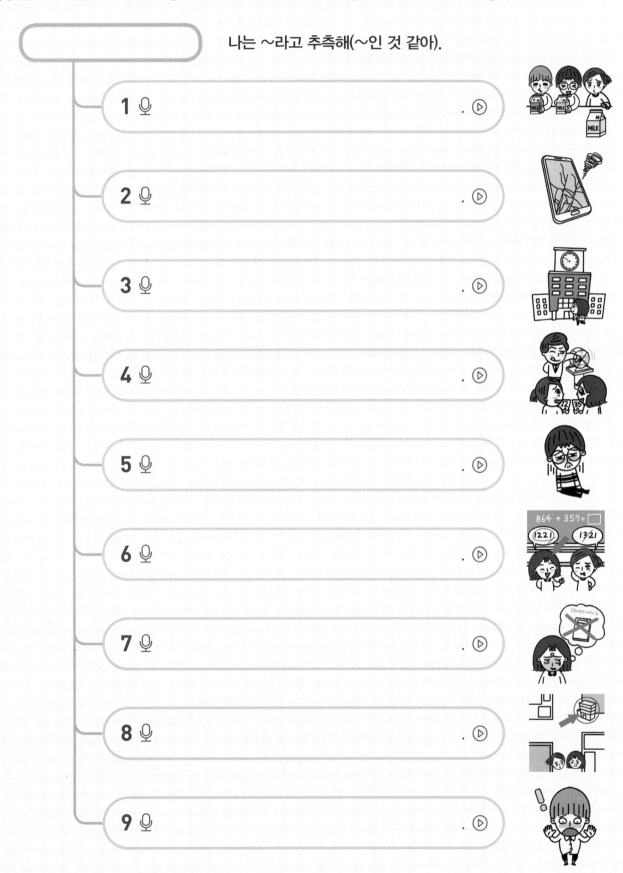

1 🎤 _____ . ▷

2 🎤 _____ . ▷

3 🎤 _____ . ▷

4 🎤 _____ . ▷

5 🎤 _____ . ▷

6 🎤 _____ . ▷

7 🎤 _____ . ▷

8 🎤 _____ . ▷

9 🎤 _____ . ▷

110
Track

I hope (that) you like this.

나는 ~하기를 바라(~하면 좋겠어).

Master words & chunks!

Ⓐ 상자 안에 있는 단어 조각들을 화살표로 연결하여 이번 트랙에서 배운 표현을 만들어 보세요.

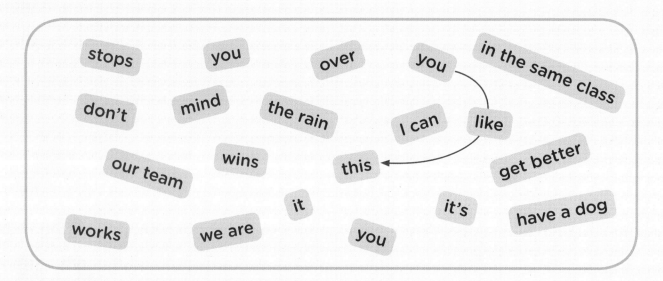

Ⓑ 상자에서 연결한 표현을 다시 한 번 써보고 뜻을 적어보세요.

Words & Chunks	뜻

Master sentences!

⭐ 앞에서 복습한 표현을 사용하여 이번 트랙에서 배운 문장을 각 그림에 맞게 완성해보세요.

나는 ～하기를 바라(～하면 좋겠어).

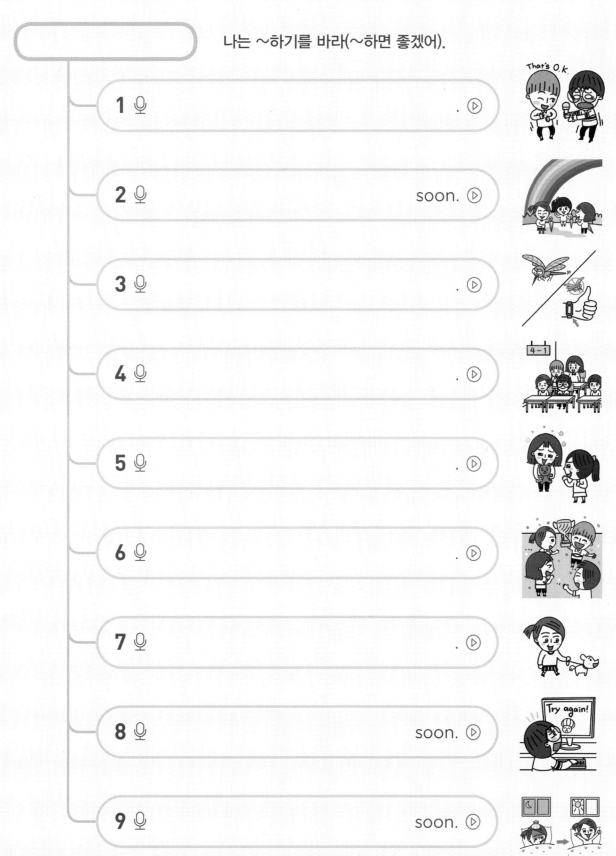

1 🎤   . ▷

2 🎤   soon. ▷

3 🎤   . ▷

4 🎤   . ▷

5 🎤   . ▷

6 🎤   . ▷

7 🎤   . ▷

8 🎤   soon. ▷

9 🎤   soon. ▷

111
Track

I'm sure (that) it was a mistake.

나는 ~라고 확신해. / 분명히 ~할 거야.

Master words & chunks!

Ⓐ 상자 안에 있는 단어 조각들을 화살표로 연결하여 이번 트랙에서 배운 표현을 만들어 보세요.

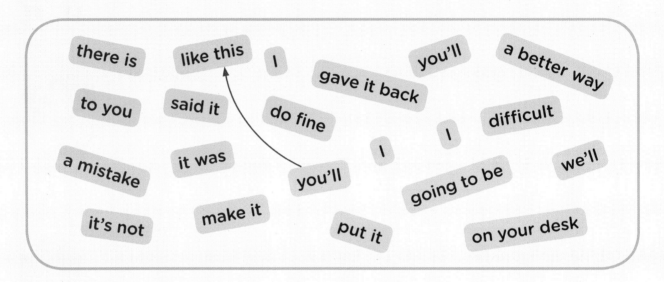

Ⓑ 상자에서 연결한 표현을 다시 한 번 써보고 뜻을 적어보세요.

Words & Chunks	뜻

Master sentences!

★ 앞에서 복습한 표현을 사용하여 이번 트랙에서 배운 문장을 각 그림에 맞게 완성해보세요.

나는 ~라고 확신해. / 분명히 ~할 거야.

1 🎤 . ▷

2 🎤 . ▷

3 🎤 . ▷

4 🎤 . ▷

5 🎤 . ▷

6 🎤 . ▷

7 🎤 . ▷

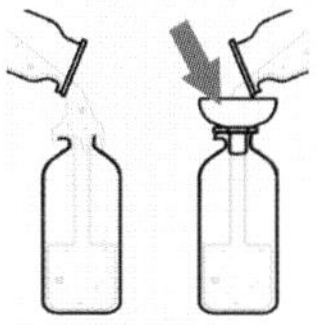

8 🎤 . ▷

9 🎤 . ▷

112
Track

That's why I'm late.

그것이 ~한 이유야(그래서 ~인 거야).

Master words & chunks!

Ⓐ 상자 안에 있는 단어 조각들을 화살표로 연결하여 이번 트랙에서 배운 표현을 만들어 보세요.

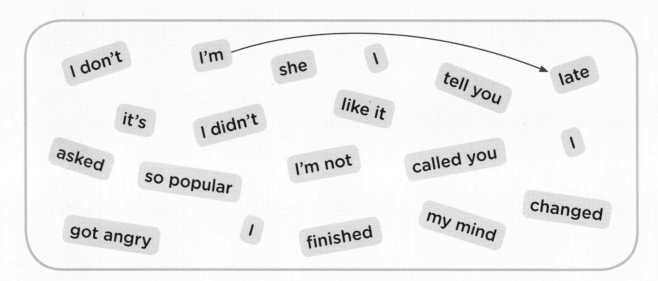

Ⓑ 상자에서 연결한 표현을 다시 한 번 써보고 뜻을 적어보세요.

Words & Chunks	뜻

Master sentences!

★ 앞에서 복습한 표현을 사용하여 이번 트랙에서 배운 문장을 각 그림에 맞게 완성해보세요.

그것이 ~한 이유야(그래서 ~인 거야).

1 🎤 _____ . ▷

2 🎤 _____ . ▷

3 🎤 _____ . ▷

4 🎤 _____ . ▷

5 🎤 _____ . ▷

6 🎤 _____ . ▷

7 🎤 _____ . ▷

8 🎤 _____ . ▷

9 🎤 _____ . ▷

초 등 코 치
천일문 시리즈

sentence [센텐스] *1,2,3,4,5*
1001개 통문장 암기로 완성하는 영어의 기초

grammar [그래머] *1,2,3*
1001개 예문으로 배우는 초등 영문법

voca&story [보카 & 스토리] *1,2*
1001개의 초등 필수 어휘와 짧은 스토리

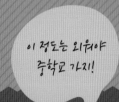

쎄듀 초등 커리큘럼

	예비초	초1	초2	초3	초4	초5	초6
구문				초등코치 천일문 SENTENCE 1001개 통문장 암기로 완성하는 초등 영어의 기초			
문법					초등코치 천일문 GRAMMAR 1001개 예문으로 배우는 초등 영문법		
문법			신간 왓츠 Grammar Start 시리즈 초등 기초 영문법 입문				
문법					신간 왓츠 Grammar Plus 시리즈 초등 필수 영문법 마무리		
독해				신간 왓츠 리딩 70 / 80 / 90 / 100 A / B 쉽고 재미있게 완성되는 영어 독해력			
어휘				초등코치 천일문 VOCA&STORY 1001개의 초등 필수 어휘와 짧은 스토리			
어휘		패턴으로 말하는 초등 필수 영단어 1 / 2 문장 패턴으로 완성하는 초등 필수 영단어					
ELT	Oh! My PHONICS 1 / 2 / 3 / 4 유·초등학생을 위한 첫 영어 파닉스						
ELT	Oh! My SPEAKING 1 / 2 / 3 / 4 / 5 / 6 핵심 문장 패턴으로 더욱 쉬운 영어 말하기						
ELT	Oh! My GRAMMAR 1 / 2 / 3 쓰기로 완성하는 첫 초등 영문법						

쎄듀 중등 커리큘럼

	예비중	중1	중2	중3
구문	신간 천일문 STARTER 1 / 2			중등 필수 구문 & 문법 총정리
문법	천일문 GRAMMAR LEVEL 1 / 2 / 3			예문 중심 문법 기본서
문법	GRAMMAR Q Starter 1, 2 / Intermediate 1, 2 / Advanced 1, 2			학기별 문법 기본서
문법	잘 풀리는 영문법 1 / 2 / 3			문제 중심 문법 적용서
문법	GRAMMAR PIC 1 / 2 / 3 / 4			이해가 쉬운 도식화된 문법서
문법			1센치 영문법	1권으로 핵심 문법 정리
문법+어법		첫단추 BASIC 문법·어법편 1 / 2		문법·어법의 기초
문법+쓰기	EGU 영단어&품사 / 문장 형식 / 동사 써먹기 / 문법 써먹기 / 구문 써먹기			서술형 기초 세우기와 문법 다지기
문법+쓰기				올씀 1 기본 문장 PATTERN 내신 서술형 기본 문장 학습
쓰기	거침없이 Writing LEVEL 1 / 2 / 3			중등 교과서 내신 기출 서술형
쓰기		개정 중학 영어 쓰작 1 / 2 / 3		중등 교과서 패턴 드릴 서술형
어휘	어휘끝 중학 필수편	중학 필수어휘 1000개	어휘끝 중학 마스터편	고난도 중학어휘 +고등기초 어휘 1000개
독해	Reading Relay Starter 1, 2 / Challenger 1, 2 / Master 1, 2			타교과 연계 배경 지식 독해
독해	READING Q Starter 1, 2 / Intermediate 1, 2 / Advanced 1, 2			예측/추론/요약 사고력 독해
독해전략			리딩 플랫폼 1 / 2 / 3	논픽션 지문 독해
독해유형		Reading 16 LEVEL 1 / 2 / 3		수능 유형 맛보기 + 내신 대비
독해유형		첫단추 BASIC 독해편 1 / 2		수능 유형 독해 입문
듣기	Listening Q 유형편 / 1 / 2 / 3			유형별 듣기 전략 및 실전 대비
듣기		쎄듀 빠르게 중학영어듣기 모의고사 1 / 2 / 3		교육청 듣기평가 대비